Green Grow the Lilacs

A Play

by Lynn Riggs

A SAMUEL FRENCH ACTING EDITION

SAMUEL FRENCH

FOUNDED 1830

New York Hollywood London Toronto

SAMUELFRENCH.COM

To
BARRETT H. CLARK

PREFACE

This reading version of *Green Grow the Lilacs* is a little fuller, a little more complete, especially in Scenes Five and Six, than the version so admirably produced by the Theatre Guild.

It must be fairly obvious from reading or seeing the play that it might have been subtitled *An Old Song*. The intent has been solely to recapture in a kind of nostalgic glow (but in dramatic dialogue more than in song) the great range of mood which characterized the old folk songs and ballads I used to hear in my Oklahoma childhood—their quaintness, their sadness, their robustness, their simplicity, their hearty or bawdy humors, their sentimentalities, their melodrama, their touching sweetness.

For this reason it seemed wise to throw away the conventions of ordinary theatricality—a complex plot, swift action, etc.—and try to exhibit luminously, in the simplest of stories, a wide area of mood and feeling. This could only be done, it seemed to me, by exploring the characters as deeply as possible, simple though they appeared to be, hoping to stumble on, if lucky, the always subtle, always strange compulsions under which they labor and relate themselves to the earth and to other people.

In the interests of this design, I thought of the first three scenes as *The Characters*, the last three scenes as *The Play*. After the people are known (and I think they are known by the end of Scene Three, or I should never permit the play to be published) I let them go ahead acting out their simple tale, which might have been the substance of an ancient song.

My beliefs anyway, I find, about the nature of true drama run counter to the current notions about it. Two people in a room, agreeing or not agreeing, are to me truly dramatic. The edges of their being can never be in accord; psychically, as well as physically, they are assailed by an opposing radiation. And the nature of the flow of spirit from each determines both the quality of their conflict, and the shape of their story. This flow may be violent or comic or tender; it may be one-sided, subtle, maddeningly recluse.

And the dramatist, it seems to me, has no business to interfere just for the sake of making a "play," in its present—and idiotic—meaning. That he may be tempted to do so is lamentable, but not surprising—the rewards are great. But if he takes his work seriously, he will face his problems in a limbo beyond the knowledge of applause. His role will continue to be humility and abnegation.

And sometime, his characters may do stirring things he could never have calculated. And sometime, if he is fortunate, he may hear from the people he has set in motion (as Shakespeare and Chekhov often heard) things to astonish him and things to make him wise.

LYNN RIGGS.

The following is a copy of the program of the first perform-
ance of "GREEN GROW THE LILACS," as produced at the Guild
Theatre, New York, Monday evening, January 26, 1931.

THE THEATRE GUILD, Inc.

PRESENTS

GREEN GROW THE LILACS

A Folk-Play in Six Scenes

By LYNN RIGGS

PRODUCTION DIRECTED BY HERBERT J. BIBERMAN
SETTINGS DESIGNED BY RAYMOND SOVEY

CAST (IN ORDER OF APPEARANCE)

CURLY McCLAIN	*Franchot Tone*
AUNT ELLER MURPHY	*Helen Westley*
LAUREY WILLIAMS	*June Walker*
JEETER FRY	*Richard Hale*
ADO ANNIE CARNES	*Ruth Chorpenning*
A PEDDLER	*Lee Strasberg*
OLD MAN PECK	*Tex Cooper*
A COWBOY	*Woodward Ritter*
ANOTHER COWBOY	*Paul Ravell*
	(*Courtesy of David Guion*)
AN OLD FARMER	*William T. Hays*
A YOUNG FARMER	*A. L. Bartolot*
MARTHY	*Jane Alden*
FIDDLER	*William Chosnyk*
BANJO PLAYER	*Everett Cheetham*
OTHER FARMERS	*Carl Beasley, Joe Wilson, Roy Ketcham, Gordon Bryant, Everett Cheetham, Elmo Carr, Tommy Pladgett.*
COWBOYS	*Slim Cavanaugh, Chick Hannan, Norton Worden, Jack Miller, Pete Schwartz, J. B. Hubbard.*
GIRLS	*Jean Wood, Lois Lindon, Orlanda Lee, Alice Frost, Faith Hope, Eleanor Powers, Peggy Hannan.*

Green Grow the Lilacs is laid in Indian Territory in 1900.
Oklahoma, which was admitted to the Union as a state in 1907,
was formed by combining Indian and Oklahoma Territories.

SYNOPSIS OF SCENES

Scene 1—The Williams' farm houses.

Scene 2—The same, showing Laurey's bedroom.

Scene 3—The same, showing the smoke house.
(The time of Scenes 2 and 3 is simultaneous)

INTERMISSION

Scene 4—The porch of Old Man Peck's house.

Scene 5—The hay-field back of Williams' house, a month
later.

Scene 6—The living-room of the Williams' house, three
nights later.

The songs in *Green Grow the Lilacs* are old and tradi-
tional. The specific acknowledgments concerning the ar-
rangements used are to:

Margaret Larkin for *Sam Hall, Hello, Girls, I Wish I
Was Single Again* and *Home on the Range*. (From her col-
lection, *Singing Cowboy*, published by Alfred A. Knopf.)

Oscar J. Fox for *Goodbye, Old Paint* (Published by
Carl Fischer).

Everett Cheetham for *Strawberry Roan* and *Blood on the
Saddle*.

The Company of *Green Grow the Lilacs* for *Chisholm
Trail* and *Next Big River*.

The other songs are from the original script of the play.

PEOPLE

CURLY MCCLAIN
AUNT ELLER MURPHY
LAUREY WILLIAMS
JEETER FRY
ADO ANNIE CARNES
A PEDLER
CORD ELAM
OLD MAN PECK
AND OTHERS OF THE COUNTRYSIDE

SCENES

SCENE 1—The "front" room of the Williams farm-house, a June morning.

SCENE 2—Laurey's bedroom.

SCENE 3—The smoke house.

SCENE 4—The porch of Old Man Peck's house, that night.

SCENE 5—The hayfield, a month later.

SCENE 6—The "front" room, three nights later.

The action of the play takes place in Indian Territory in 1900.

SCENE ONE

It is a radiant summer morning several years ago, the kind of morning which, enveloping the shapes of earth —men, cattle in a meadow, blades of the young corn, streams—makes them seem to exist now for the first time, their images giving off a visible golden emanation that is partly true and partly a trick of imagination focussing to keep alive a loveliness that may pass away.

The unearthly sunlight pours through the crocheted curtains of a window in the living room—the "front room"—of a farm house in Indian Territory. It rests upon, and glorifies, scrubbed floors of oak, bright rag rugs, rough hide-bottomed hairy chairs, a rock fireplace, a settee, an old organ magnificently mirrored, ancestral enlargements in their gilt and oval frames. A double sliding door of pine, now closed, is at the back of the room; other heavier doors of oak lead to other parts of the house and to the outside. Somewhere a dog barks twice and stops quickly, reassured; a turkey gobbler makes his startled, swallowing noise.

And, like the voice of the morning, a rich male voice outside somewhere begins to sing:

VOICE

As I walked out one bright sunny morning,
I saw a cowboy way out on the plain.
His hat was throwed back and his spurs was a-jingling,
And as I passed by him, he was singing this refrain:

3

Ta whoop ti aye ay, git along, you little dogies!
Way out in Wyoming shall be your bright home—
A-whooping and a-yelling and a-driving those dogies,
And a-riding those bronchos that are none of my own.

The people all say we're goin' to have a picnic,
But I tell you, my boy, they've got 'er down wrong,
For 'f it hadn't a-been for those troublesome dogies,
I never woulda thought of composing this song.

Ta whoop ti aye ay, git along, you little dogies!
Way out in Wyoming shall be your bright home—
A-whooping and a-yelling and a-driving those dogies,
And a-riding those bronchos that are none of my own.

[*Before the first verse is finished, part of the singer
comes into sight at a window—a tall, waggish, curly-
headed young cowboy in a checked shirt and a ten-
gallon hat. He looks about the room singing. Just as
he finishes he withdraws, hearing footsteps. A moment
later,* AUNT ELLER MURPHY, *a buxom, hearty woman
about fifty, with a tall wooden brass-banded churn in
her arms, comes in from the kitchen. She puts the
churn down quickly by the fireplace, goes over to the
window and looks out, squinting. She grins, good-
humoredly.*

AUNT ELLER

Oh, I see you, Mr. Curly McClain! Don't need to be
a-hidin' 'hind that horse of your'n. Couldn't hide them
feet of your'n even if yer head wasn't showin'. So you
may as well come on in.

[*She turns away from the window, takes off her apron, and comes back into the room.* CURLY *appears again at the window.*

CURLY

Hi, Aunt Eller.

AUNT ELLER (*shortly*)

Skeer me to death! Whut're you doin' around here?

CURLY

Come a-singin' to you only you never give me no time to finish.
[*Their speech is lazy, drawling, not Southern, not "hick"—but rich, half-conscious of its rhythms, its picturesque imagery.*

AUNT ELLER

Go on and finish then. (*She smiles at him.*) You do sing purty, Curly.

CURLY

Nobody never said I didn't.

AUNT ELLER

Yeah, purty. If I wasn't an old womern, and if you wasn't so young and smart-alecky—why, I'd marry you and git you to set around at night and sing to me.

CURLY

No, you wouldn't, neither. If I was to marry—any-one—I wouldn't set around at night a-singin'. They ain't no tellin' *whut* I'd do. But I wouldn't marry you ner none of yer kinfolks, I could he'p it.

AUNT ELLER (*wisely*)

Oh! None of my kinfolks neither, huh?

CURLY

And you c'n tell 'em that, *all* of 'em, includin' that niece of your'n, Miss Laurey Williams, if she's about anywhurs.

AUNT ELLER

Mebbe I will, and mebbe I won't. Whut you doin' over this-a-way, Curly? Thought you was over at Skid-more's ranch, tother side of Justus. Well, air you comin' in or gonna stay there like a Jack-in-the-box? [CURLY *vaults into the room. He wears dark trousers stuffed into high boots. His heavy rowelled spurs clink against the floor.*

CURLY (*deliberately*)

Aunt Eller, if you was to tell me whur Laurey was at —*whur* would you tell me she was at?

AUNT ELLER

I wouldn't tell you a-tall, less'n you sung me another song.

CURLY

Must think I'm a medicine man a-singin' and passin' the hat around, the way you talk! Got to save my voice, got to take keer of it, so I'll have it. Don't want to do the way ole man Comer done. When he was a kid he squalled so much, and when he was growed he sung so much, now he's a ole man he cain't git a squawk out of him, nary a squawk. 'Cept a whistle. And a whistle don't mean nuthin'—the way a song do.

AUNT ELLER (*unimpressed*)

Sing me a song, Curly McClain.

CURLY

Aw, I *cain't* sing now! I *told* you. Not if I tried and tried, and even et cat-gut. And even 'f I drunk the gall of a turkey gobbler's liver, I couldn't sing a-tall.

AUNT ELLER

Liar and a hypocrite and a shikepoke! Ain't I heared you? Jist now. *You sing!* Er I'll run you off the place.

CURLY

I cain't sing, I told you! 'Ceptin' when I'm lonesome. Out in the saddle when it ain't so sunny, er on a dark night close to a fa'r when you feel so lonesome to God you could die. Looky here, you're old, my, you're old, you'd orter be so smart! Whur you been, anyhow, whose side meat you been eatin' all yer life, not to know nobody cain't sing good 'ceptin' when he's lonesome?

AUNT ELLER

Lonesome? Then if I was you I'd be a-singin' and a-singin' then. A long song, with forty 'leven verses and a chorus 'tween ever' verse. Fer as fur as I c'n make out, Laurey ain't payin' you no heed a-tall. You might jist as well be ridin' the rails as ridin' that range of your'n. So sing yer head off, you lonesome dogie, 'cause you shore have got into a lonesome side-pocket 'thout no grass, you dehorned maverick, you!

CURLY

Whut'd I keer about that?

[*He takes cigaret papers out of his hat-band, Bull*

Durham from his shirt pocket, and begins to roll a cigaret, with elaborate unconcern.

AUNT ELLER

She goes around with her head some'eres else, don't she?

CURLY

How'd I know? Ain't looked at her nary a time since Christmas.

AUNT ELLER

'Twasn't yore fault though, if you didn't. (*Jeering, good-naturedly.*) She don't see you, does she, Mr. Adam's Off Ox! You've got onto the wrong side of the wagon tongue!

CURLY

Go on, you mean ole womern! Brand a steer till you burn a hole in his hide!

AUNT ELLER

Mr. Cowboy! A-ridin' high, wide and handsome, his spurs a-jinglin', and the Bull Durham tag a-whippin' outa his pocket! Oh, *Mr.* Cowpuncher! 'Thout no home, ner no wife, ner no one to muss up his curly hair, er keep him warm on a winter's night!

CURLY (*swelling up, defensively*)

So she don't take to me much, huh? Whur'd you git sich a uppity niece 'at wouldn't pay no heed to *me?* Who's the best bronc buster in this yere state?

AUNT ELLER

You, I bet.

CURLY

And the best bull-dogger in seventeen counties? *Me,* that's who! And looky here, I'm handsome, ain't I?

AUNT ELLER

Purty as a pitcher.

CURLY

Curly-headed, ain't I? And bow-legged from the saddle fer God knows how long, ain't I?

AUNT ELLER (*agreeing*)

Couldn't stop a pig in the road.

CURLY

Well, whut else does she want then, the damn she-mule?

AUNT ELLER

I don't know. But I'm shore sartin it ain't *you.*

CURLY

Anh! Quit it, you'll have me a-cryin'!

AUNT ELLER (*triumphantly*)

You better sing me a song then, like I told you to in the first place!

CURLY

Aw, whut'll I sing then?

AUNT ELLER

"A-ridin' ole Paint."

CURLY

And nen whut'll I sing?

AUNT ELLER

Lands, you better git one sung 'fore you start in on another'n!

[*But* CURLY *has already leaned against the wall with his head thrown back, and his feet crossed, and begun to sing in his rich, liquid, mock-heroic voice.*

CURLY (*singing*)

A-ridin' ole Paint and a-leadin' old Dan,
I'm goin' to Montana for to throw the hoolian.
They feed in the hollers and they water in the draw,
Their tails are all matted and their backs are all raw.

Ride around the little dogies, ride around them slow,
For the fiery and the snuffy are a-rarin' to go.

Ole Bill Jones had two daughters and a son,
One went to Denver and the other went wrong,
One was killed in a pool room fight,
But still he goes singing from morn till night:

Ride around the little dogies, ride around them slow,
For the fiery and the snuffy are a-rarin' to go.

When I die take my saddle from the wall,
Put it on my pony, lead him out of his stall,
Tie my bones to the saddle, turn our faces to the west,
And we'll ride the trail that we love best.

Ride around the little dogies, ride around them slow,
For the fiery and the snuffy are a-rarin' to go.

Now whur's Laurey at?

AUNT ELLER (*pointing*)

Settin' in there in her room a-sewin' 'er sump'n, when she orta be in here a-churnin' like I told her. Ain't you gonna sing another song?

CURLY

Ain't you a bother though—keep on a-pesterin'! You go and tell Laurey to drop a stitch, and see whut Sandy Claus brung her.

AUNT ELLER

Meanin' you, I guess. Whut'd you want with her, Curly, nohow? I'm her aunt, so you better tell me first, and see if I like the looks of it.

CURLY

You're jist nosy. Well, if you have to know my business, ole man Peck over acrost Dog Crick's givin' a play-party and I come to ast if Laurey ud go with me.

AUNT ELLER

And me, too, huh?

CURLY

Yeow, you too. If you'll go and knock on the door there, and bring Laurey out whur a man c'n git a look at her.

AUNT ELLER (*knocking*)

Laurey! Peck's is givin' a play-party.

LAUREY (*inside*)

Who's givin' a play-party?

AUNT ELLER

Ole man Peck acrost Dog Crick.

LAUREY

Cain't hear a word you say. Who?

AUNT ELLER (*shouting*)

Come on out. Someone's come to see you. He'll tell you.

LAUREY

Who's come to see me? Who's givin' a party?

AUNT ELLER

Well, open up the door, you crazy youngun, I cain't holler my head off!
[*The door slides back, and* LAUREY *comes out. She is a fair, spoiled, lovely young girl about eighteen in a long white dress with many ruffles. She sees* CURLY.

LAUREY

Oh! Thought you was somebody. (*To* AUNT ELLER.) Is this all that's come a-callin' and it a'ready ten o'clock of a Satiddy mornin'?

CURLY (*sullenly*)

You knowed it was me 'fore you opened the door.

LAUREY

No sich of a thing.

CURLY

You did, too! You heared my voice and knowed it was me.

LAUREY

I did not, I tell you! Heared a voice a-talkin' rumbly
along with Aunt Eller. And heared someone a-singin'
like a bull-frog in a pond—

CURLY

I don't talk rumbly. And I don't sing like no bull-
frog—

LAUREY

Bull-frog in a pond, I told you. But how'd I know it
was you, Mr. Curly McClain? You ain't so special.
All men sounds alike to me.

CURLY (*doggedly*)

You knowed it was me, so you set in there a-thinkin'
up sump'n mean to say. I'm a good mind not to tell
you nuthin' about the play-party now. You c'n jist
stay at home, for yer tongue. Don't you tell her whur
it is, Aunt Eller. Me'n you'll go and leave her at
home.

LAUREY

If you *did* ast me, I wouldn't go with you. Besides,
how'd you take me? You ain't bought a new buggy
with red wheels onto it, have you?

CURLY

No, I ain't.

LAUREY

And a spankin' team with their bridles all jinglin'?

CURLY

No.

LAUREY

'Spect me to ride on behind ole Dun, I guess. You better ast that ole Cummins girl you've tuck sich a shine to, over acrost the river.

CURLY

If I was to ast you, they'd be a way to take you, Miss Laurey Smarty.

LAUREY

Oh, they would?

CURLY

A bran' new surrey with fringe on the top four inches long—and *yeller!* And two white horses a-rarin' and faunchin' to go! You'd shore ride like a queen settin' up in *that* carriage! Feel like you had a gold crown set on yer head, 'th diamonds in it big as goose eggs.

LAUREY

Look out, you'll be astin' me in a minute!

CURLY

I ain't astin' you, I'm *tellin'* you. And this yere rig has got four fine side-curtains, case of a rain. And isinglass winders to look out of! And a red and green lamp set on the dashboard, winkin' like a lightnin' bug!

LAUREY

Whur'd you git sich a rig at? (*With explosive laughter.*) Anh, I bet he's went and h'ard it over to Claremore, thinkin' I'd go with him!

CURLY

'S all you know about it—

LAUREY (*jeering*)

Went and h'ard it! Spent all his money h'arin' a rig, and now ain't got nobody to ride in it.

CURLY

Have, too! Did *not* h'ar it. Made the whole thing up outa my head—

LAUREY

What! Made it up?

CURLY

Dashboard and all!

LAUREY (*flying at him*)

Oh! Git outa the house, you! Aunt Eller, make him git hisself outa here 'fore I take a stove arn to him! Tellin' me lies—!

CURLY (*dodging her*)

Makin' up a few— Look out, now! Makin' up a few purties ain't agin no law 'at I know of. Don't you wish they *was* sich a rig, though? Nen you could go to the party and do a hoe-down till mornin' 'f you was a mind to. Nen drive home 'th the sun a-peekin' at you over the ridge, purty and fine.

LAUREY

I ain't wantin' to do no hoe-down till mornin'. And whut would I want to see the sun come up fer, a-peekin' purty and fine—alongside of you, anyhow?

AUNT ELLER

Whyn't you jist grab her and kiss her when she acts that-a-way, Curly? She's jist achin' fer you to, I bet.

LAUREY (*with mock fury*)

Oh! I won't even *speak* to him, let alone 'low him to kiss me, the braggin', saddle-awk'ard, wish-'t-he-had-a-sweetheart bum!
[*She flounces into her room, and bangs the sliding door.*

AUNT ELLER (*turning to* CURLY, *sagely*)

She likes you—quite a little.

CURLY

Whew! 'F she liked me quite a *lot*, she'd sic the dogs onto me, or shoot me full of buckshot!

AUNT ELLER

No, come 'ere, Curly, while I tell you sump'n. A womern that won't let you tetch her 'th a ten foot pole like that is jist dyin' fer you to git closer'n *that* to her.

CURLY

Mebbe. But they's women and women. And some of 'em is accordin' to the rules, and some of 'em ain't never *heared* no rules to be accordin' *to*. Guess I better be movin' my camp some'eres else.

AUNT ELLER

No, look here, Curly. I've knowed Laurey all her born days, ain't I? And since her paw and maw died five year ago, I been paw and maw both to her. And whutever I tell you about her way of feelin' is the truth. Er if it *ain't*, I'll give her a everlastin' good spankin', nen it *will* be! Fer I don't know whur her eyes was set in her head 'f she didn't see you, you purty thing, right from the start, the time you come over of a Sunday a year ago and broke them three broncs all in one evenin', 'thout tetchin' leather er yellin' calf-rope. 'Member?

CURLY (*feeling a little better*)

Yeah, I remember. Mean as sin they was, too! That one-eyed un 'th the star in his forehead liked to set me over his head right smack into them lilac bushes the first crack outa the bucket, didn't he? Yeah, onct I break 'em, they're purty apt to stay broke, fer a fact. (*Cryptically.*) You c'n *count* on a horse. (*Suddenly.*) Look here, Aunt Eller, I wanta know sump'n and if you lie to me, I'll ketch thirteen bulgy-eyed toad-frogs and put 'em in yer bed—

AUNT ELLER

Laws a-mercy!

CURLY

Er make you chew Indian turnip till yer tongue feels like a thousand needles run through it, and no way of pullin' 'em out—

AUNT ELLER

Feel 'em a'ready.

CURLY

Listen, whut low, filthy, sneakin' man has Laurey got her cap set fer?

AUNT ELLER

You.

CURLY

Now!—

AUNT ELLER

Fer a fact, I'm tellin' you! From the way she flew at you jist now, I got my mind all made up. 'F she don't git *you*, Curly, she'll waste away to the shadder of a pin point. Yes, sir. Be put in a sateen coffin dead of a broke heart.

CURLY (*ironically*)

I wouldn't want her to do *that*. I'd consider lettin' her *have* me, 'f that ud keep her from dyin'.

AUNT ELLER (*wisely*)

She's a young girl—and don't know her mind. She don't know her feelin's. You c'n he'p her, Curly— and they's few that can.

CURLY

They must be plenty of men a-tryin' to spark her. And she shorely leans to one of 'em, now don't she?

AUNT ELLER

Ain't no one a-sparkin' her. Well, they is that ole widder man at Claremore, makes out he's a doctor er a vet'nary. And that fine farmer, Jace Hutchins, jist this side of Lone Ellum—

CURLY

That's whut I thought!

AUNT ELLER

Not to say nuthin' about someone nearer home that's
got her on his mind most of the time, till he don't
know a plow from a thrashin' machine—

CURLY

Who'd you mean by that?

AUNT ELLER

Jeeter.

CURLY

Jeeter who?

AUNT ELLER

Don't you know Jeeter Fry, our h'ard hand?

CURLY

What! That bullet-colored growly man 'th the bushy
eyebrows that's alwys orderin' the other hands how
to work the mowin' machine er sump'n!

AUNT ELLER

Now you don't need to go and say nuthin' agin
him! He's a big help around here. Jist about runs
the farm by hisself. Well, two women couldn't do it,
you orta know that.

CURLY

Laurey'd take up 'th a man like that!

AUNT ELLER

I ain't said she's tuck up with him.

CURLY

Well, he's around all the time, ain't he? Eats his meals with you like one of the fambly, don't he? Sleeps around here some'eres, don't he?

AUNT ELLER

Out in the smoke-house.

CURLY

Laurey sees him all the time, then, don't she? Whyn't you say so in the first place! Whur is this Jeeter, till I git a look at him and mebbe olack his eyes fer him?

AUNT ELLER (*slyly*)

Thought you'd moved yer camp some'eres else?

CURLY (*with exaggerated bravado*)

My camp's right here till I git ready to break it. And moreover—whoever puts his foot in it's liable to git shot fer a stinkin' skunk er a sneakin' wildcat!
[*As if waiting for this declaration, the front door bangs open, and the bullet-colored, growly man, with an armful of wood for the fireplace, comes in. He throws the wood in the wood-box, and turns to* AUNT ELLER.

JEETER

Whur's Laurey at?

AUNT ELLER

In her room there.
[*JEETER gives a surly grunt by way of response,*

and without another word goes out again, leaving the door wide open behind him.

CURLY

Now is that Jeeter?

AUNT ELLER

Yeah.

CURLY

Thought it was. (*He goes over and looks out after him.*) Why ain't he a-workin'?

AUNT ELLER

It's Satiddy.

CURLY

Oh! I'd forgot. He's went in the smoke-house.

AUNT ELLER

It's *his* house. Used to be the *dog*-house.

CURLY (*chuckling*)

That's the place fer him!
[*The sliding door opens a crack, and* LAUREY *sticks her head out.*

LAUREY

I forgot to tell you, Aunt Eller, you'll have to do the churnin' yerself, less'n you c'n git someone to do it fer you.

AUNT ELLER

Why, you lazy youngun, I'll do no sich of a thing! I got dinner on the stove—

LAUREY

It takes time fer a girl to git herself fixed up, it looks to me like. I'm goin' to a party tonight.

AUNT ELLER

To a party?

LAUREY

Well, stand there 'th yer mouth open! Didn't I tell you?—At ole man Peck's over acrost Dog Crick.

AUNT ELLER

Now whoever went and— Did you, Curly?

LAUREY

I heared about it a week ago. Jeeter told me. I'm goin' with Jeeter.
[*She withdraws.* CURLY *stands very still.*

CURLY (*after a moment*)

Ever hear that song, Aunt Eller?

AUNT ELLER (*frowning*)

A thousand pins it takes 'em to dress—

CURLY (*grins, ruefully*)

Now wouldn't that jist make you bawl!
[*He goes over, touches a few chords on the organ soberly, and then recovering, seats himself, and after a moment begins to sing, half-satirically. But by the time he has reached the first chorus, the song with its absurd yet plaintive charm has absorbed him. And he sings the rest of its sentimental periods, his head back, his eyes focussed beyond the room, be-*

*yond himself—upon the young man having his sad
say, the young man who'll go into the army, by God,
and put an end to his distemper, his unrequited
fervor.*

CURLY (*singing*)

I used to have a sweetheart, but now I've got none,
Since she's gone and left me, I care not for one,
Since she's gone and left me, contented I'll be,
For she loves another one better than me.

Green grow the lilacs, all sparkling with dew,
I'm lonely, my darling, since parting with you,
And by the next meeting I hope to prove true
To change the green lilacs to the red, white and blue.

I passed my love's window, both early and late,
The look that she gave me, it made my heart ache,
The look that she gave me was harmful to see,
For she loves another one better than me.

Green grow the lilacs, all sparkling with dew,
I'm lonely, my darling, since parting with you,
And by the next meeting I hope to prove true
To change the green lilacs to the red, white and blue.

I wrote my love a letter in red rosy lines,
She sent me an answer all twisted in twines,
Saying "Keep your love letters and I will keep mine,
Just write to your sweetheart and I'll write to mine."

Green grow the lilacs, all sparkling with dew,
I'm lonely, my darling, since parting with you.

And by the next meeting I hope to prove true
To change the green lilacs to the red, white and blue.

[*He swings off the organ stool, miraculously healed,
and makes for the door.*

AUNT ELLER (*following him over*)
Now don't you be discouraged none, Curly. Laurey's
good. She's got sense. She don't let you know too
much—keeps you guessin'. And you shore got *her*
to wonderin', too! You're shore a pair—full of life—
made for each other! Got to have each other. *Got* to.
(*She laughs.*) Thought I'd die when you made up
all that about the rig and told her—

CURLY (*whistles softly*)
Jesus! (*He turns round with a grin.*) Well, we got
a date together, you and me, Aunt Eller.

AUNT ELLER
We have?

CURLY
We shore have. We goin' to that party we've heared
so much about.

AUNT ELLER
How we goin', Curly? In that rig you made up?
(*She chuckles.*) I'll ride a-straddle of them lights
a-winkin' like lightnin' bugs, myself!

CURLY
That there rig ain't no made-up rig, you hear me?
I h'ard it over to Claremore.

AUNT ELLER

Lands, you did!

CURLY

And when I come callin' fer you right after supper, see that you got yer beauty spots fastened onto you proper, so you won't lose 'em off, you hear? Now then. (*He strides away to the door again, enigmatically.*) I think I'll jist go out here to the smoke-house a while.

AUNT ELLER (*puzzled*)

Whur Jeeter's at?

CURLY

Yeow, whur Jeeter's at. Thought mebbe I'd play a game of pitch with him, 'fore I mosey on home. You reckon he'd like that?

[*He goes out the door.* AUNT ELLER *stares after him, figuring out things.*

CURTAIN

SCENE TWO

LAUREY's *bedroom, behind its sliding doors is small, primitive, but feminine. There's a bed, covered with a beautiful crazy-quilt, a dresser, very ornate, with little souvenir shell boxes, combs, hair receivers, hair-pins, a vase of buttercups and daisies, etc. There's a small table with pitchers of water under it, and comfortable chairs. A small window looks out into the brilliant day. At the left is a door which goes out to the swept yard in front of the kitchen. The walls are papered, and several small photographs are tacked up—one of a man on horseback, obviously for the first time, one of a young girl with enormous sleeves in her dress.*

LAUREY *is combing her hair. She seems, in this setting, younger, more glowing, more complete than before, as if the room were necessary to her. It is immediately after Scene One.* AUNT ELLER *has come in from the door at the left to see what* LAUREY *is up to.*

AUNT ELLER

Is that all you got to do?

LAUREY (*abstractedly*)

When I was a little girl I had my hair in pig-tails. It hung down and down, till I'd wrap it around my head. Nen I'd look like sump'n crawled out of a hole.

AUNT ELLER

I ain't got time to listen to sich craziness.

LAUREY

When I got a little older, I cut it off. Maw licked me.

AUNT ELLER

Well, she'd orta licked you.

LAUREY

Why?

AUNT ELLER

Fer cuttin' yer hair off. Don't you know that ain't right?

LAUREY

I ast you fer a answer and all I git is another question.

AUNT ELLER

Oh, I'm goin' back in the kitchen. You ain't started on that churnin'. I jist come in to see what you was up to so long. Here I find you a-primpin' and a-talkin' crazy.

LAUREY

Wait a minute. Why don't you set down here a minute?

AUNT ELLER

They's work to do. Ain't time to set.

LAUREY

Then redd up that table if you won't set. And put some fresh water onto them flowers I picked day be-

fore yistiddy. Them buttercups. In the meader back
of the wheat field—walkin' in the tall grass and the
sumakes, you know what I seen? A snake 'th its tail
in its mouth—

AUNT ELLER

And a terrapin carryin' a elephant, too, didn't you?

LAUREY

Won't hurt you none to put some water on them
flowers.

AUNT ELLER (*acquiescing, judicially*)

Well. You ain't always so lazy, I must say.

LAUREY

Dance at yer weddin'.

AUNT ELLER

I don't know whut's got into you, though.

LAUREY

You don't?

AUNT ELLER (*wisely*)

Yes, I do.

LAUREY (*cryptically*)

I thought you did.
[*Silence.* AUNT ELLER *fills the vase.* LAUREY *combs her
hair slowly, and begins to sing.*

One morning as I rambled o'er
The fields I took my way
In hopes of meeting my miner boy
And for a while to stray,

In hopes of meeting my miner boy,
My hope, my joy, my own.
My heart was blessed, it could find no rest
For the thoughts of my miner boy.

The mother to her daughter,
"I'll comfort you to your room,
You never shall marry a miner boy,
It will certainly be your doom.
They're never, never satisfied,
But always on a drunk.
And all they have in this wide wide world
Is a satchel and a trunk."

The daughter to her mother,
"What makes you be unkind?
I never shall marry another one
But the one that suits my mind.
His trousers are made of corduroy,
His jacket of true blue.
I'd rather marry a miner boy
As to reign with the waters true."

Then fill your glasses to the brim,
Let's all go merry round,
And drink to the health of the miner boy
Who works down in the ground,
When work is o'er comes whistling home
With a heart so full of joy,
And happy, happy is the girl
That marries a miner boy.

Would you marry a miner boy, Aunt Eller?

AUNT ELLER

I don't know no miner boys.

LAUREY

Oh, 'f you did, you would, I bet. (*After a moment.*) Wish 't I lived in the White House, and had diamonds on my shoes, and a little nigger boy to fan me—when it was hot. Does it git hot in the White House, Aunt Eller?

AUNT ELLER

How do I know?

LAUREY

Er I wish 't I lived in Virginia or Californie. In Californie, they's oranges growin', and snow fallin' at the same time. I seen a pitcher of it. In the Verdigree bottom the other day, a man found thirty-three arrow heads—thirty-three—whur they'd been a Indian battle—

AUNT ELLER

Whut's that got to do with the White House and livin' in Californie?

LAUREY

Who said anything about Californie?

AUNT ELLER (*whistles*)

Land's alive! (*After a moment.*) Curly's out in the smoke-house.

LAUREY

Who is?

AUNT ELLER

Curly. Him and Jeeter.

LAUREY (*as if she hadn't heard*)

Bet they'll be a hundred people at Peck's. They'll come in buggies and surries, a-horseback, in the wagon, and some'll come afoot. Gracie Denham will come all the way from Catoosie to be there, I bet. When she married Dan Denham, everbody thought—"Goodbye, good times"—fer Gracie. She fooled 'em, though. How big is Indian Territory, Aunt Eller?

AUNT ELLER

Oh, big.

LAUREY

It's a funny place to live, ain't it?

AUNT ELLER

Whut's funny about it?

LAUREY

Well, take me, if paw and maw hadn't come here, I'd a-been livin' in Missouri now, 'stid of here. I'd a-had education, I'll bet. (*She puts down her comb and stares thoughtfully out the window.*) I lied about the White House, Aunt Eller. I'd ruther be married to a man—if he was a real good man—than to live in the old White House.

AUNT ELLER (*chuckling*)

Hope you do one of the two!

LAUREY

Wouldn't you, Aunt Eller?

AUNT ELLER

I've done about all the marryin' I'm gonna do. Onct is quite a plenty. (*She chortles with delight.*) Less'n I marry Curly and bring him up right. Me and Curly, we're a-goin to that there party—

LAUREY (*jumps up, runs over and begins shaking the astounded* AUNT ELLER)

You ain't, you air not! He ain't got no way to take you to no party. You got to go with Jeeter and me—

AUNT ELLER

Curly's h'ard a rig. That un he told you about. (LAUREY *drops her hands, backs away, and looks at* AUNT ELLER *with such an amazed and startled expression, that the older woman cries out:*) Why, you look so funny!—Like you'd saw sump'n. (LAUREY *goes over to the window, hangs on to the curtains.*) Besides, you turned him down. (*Teasing her.*) If you jist *got* to go with Jeeter, they ain't no way out of it, I reckon. Well, me'n Curly, we'll make out—

LAUREY (*quietly, strangely*)

Onct I passed by a farm house and it was night. Paw and maw and me was in a covered wagon on our way to here. And this farm house was burnin' up. It was burnin' bright, too. Black night, it was like I said. Flames licked and licked at the red-hot chimbley and finally it fell, too, and that was the last of that house. And that was turrible! I cried and cried. (*A sudden slightly-hysterical note in her voice.*) And the farmer's wife jist set there by the side of the road, moanin' and takin' on. Had on a sunbonnet, a *sunbonnet*, and it night! She kept sayin' over and over—"Now my home's burnt up. 'F I'd jist a-give him a piece of cold pork or sump'n. If I'd jist a-fed him!—" (*She shakes her head, as if shutting it out.*) Now ain't that silly!—Don't you listen to a word I said. Ever onct in a while sump'n makes me think about it, the way that womern cried, and said whut she did. Don't you pay no attention to me—

AUNT ELLER

I b'lieve to my soul you got sump'n worryin' on yer mind. Never seen you ack before like a chicken 'th its head cut off, Laurey.

LAUREY (*flippantly*)

Worried to death.

AUNT ELLER

Whut about? Now tell yer ole Aunt. Whut is it, honey?

LAUREY

Ain't got a thing to wear tonight.

AUNT ELLER

You make me so mad—!

LAUREY

Well, I ain't. That ole flowered dew-dad of a dress looks like sump'n the cat drug in. And my sash is tore. Sylvie Roberts has got a new kind of a shoe with high heels onto 'em like stilts—and I ain't got none.

AUNT ELLER

You'd shore look purty a-wearin' stilts—like a sand-hill crane a-wadin' shaller water! That ain't whut's a-worryin' you, though—

LAUREY

I thought it was. Listen to that mockin' bird a-singin'! Ever' mornin' he sets in that ellum and sings like a tree full of birds all by hisself.

AUNT ELLER

He's lonesome.

LAUREY

He's hungry.

AUNT ELLER

Well, it's the same thing.

LAUREY (*with real passion*)

If we ever had to leave this here place, Aunt Eller, I'd shore miss it. I like it. I like that thicket down by the branch whur the 'possums live, don't you? And the way we set around in the evenings in thrashin' time, a-eatin' mushmelons and singin', and oh! lots of things! Runnin' to the cellar in a storm, and them yeller trumpet tomaters even, you make jam out of, and the branch and the pond to skate on— They's only one thing I don't to say *like*. And that's Sunday in fall, when it's windy, and the sun shines, and

the leaves piles up thick agin the house. I'm 'fraid
of my life to go from here to the kitchen—like sump'n
was gonna ketch me!

AUNT ELLER

Well, you *air* a silly.

LAUREY

But I'd shore hate to leave here, though, and go
some'eres else—like to a town or some place—

AUNT ELLER

Well, the ole Scratch! Whut makes you keep talkin'
about leavin' here?

LAUREY

Whut if we had to?

AUNT ELLER

Won't have to. We got money in the bank.

LAUREY

Bank might break.

AUNT ELLER

Well, let it. It's gonna be another good year fer
corn and oats, like it's been now fer three year—

LAUREY

Whut if sump'n happened?

AUNT ELLER

Like whut?

LAUREY

Oh, things change. Things don't last the way they
air. Besides, whut if they'd be a prairie f'ar—like

the one that burnt up a thousand acres by Chambers
School House five year ago?

AUNT ELLER

Ain't apt to be no prairie f'ar.

LAUREY

Or a cyclone ud come, like that un did at Sweetwater.
Made hash outa three whole sections.

AUNT ELLER

Cain't stop a cyclone by worryin'.

LAUREY

No? Well, whut if Jeeter ud set the house on f'ar?

AUNT ELLER

Jeeter set the— Whut in the name of Jerusalem air
you talkin' about! Jeeter set the— My goodness,
git yer things ready, gonna start you right off to
Vinita to the crazy house!

LAUREY

Well, I told you, anyway—

AUNT ELLER

Git 'em ready!

LAUREY

You don't have to listen.

AUNT ELLER

Whut if I'd put rat poison in the turnip greens?
Now whut on earth would Jeeter want to set the
house on f'ar fer?

LAUREY

I jist said he might.

AUNT ELLER

Might take a notion to rope a freight train, too. Fiddlesticks! I got my dinner on the stove a-cookin'. (*She makes for the door, slows her pace, and turns around again.*) Now, whut do you mean, anyway— Jeeter set the house on f'ar?—

LAUREY

They's a horse and buggy turnin' off up the road this-a-way.

AUNT ELLER

I won't look till you tell me whut you're a-meanin'.

LAUREY

It's a roan horse 'th a long tail. He's string-haltered. Look at the way he walks—

AUNT ELLER

Not *gonna* look, I tell you!

LAUREY

You know whut a f'ar is, don't you? And you know Jeeter?

AUNT ELLER

That's jist it.

LAUREY (*gravely, queerly*)

Sump'n funny about him. Sump'n black a-pilin' up. Ever since a year ago. Sump'n boilin' up inside of him—*mean.*

AUNT ELLER (*relieved*)

Is that it! Well, I guess you don't mind that so much —goin' to parties with him, and all.

LAUREY (*her face white—in a low voice*)

I'm afraid to tell him I won't, Aunt Eller. 'F I done what I wanted to, I'd f'ar him off the place so quick! Whut're we gonna do, Aunt Eller! He'd do sump'n turrible, he makes me shiver ever' time he gits close to me— (*With a frightened look around, as if he were in the room.*) Have you ever looked out there in the smoke-house—whur he sleeps?

AUNT ELLER

Course I have, plenty of times.

LAUREY

Whut'd you see?

AUNT ELLER

Nuthin'—but a lot of dirt. Why, whut's out there?

LAUREY (*her voice tight with excitement—creating it*)

I don't know, sump'n awful. I hook my door at night and fasten the winders agin it. Agin *it*—and the sound of feet a-walkin' up and down out there under that tree, and around the corner of the house, and down by the barn—and in the front room there!

AUNT ELLER

Laurey!

LAUREY (*as before*)

I wake up and hear the boards creakin', I tell you! The rafters jist over my head here shakes a little—

easy. Next mornin', he comes to his breakfast and looks at me out from under his eyebrows like sump'n back in the bresh some'eres. I know what I'm talkin' about—

AUNT ELLER

Why, I didn't have an idy you felt that-a-way about him! Why, we'll run him off the place if you're skeered of him—

LAUREY (*with deep premonition*)

Don't you do it! Don't you say nuthin' to him! *That's* whut skeers me—he'd do sump'n, I tell you! He'd set the house on f'ar, like I told you!

AUNT ELLER

Land's sakes! Jist let me ketch him at it! (*She laughs.*) Now you've went and made all this up, and I don't believe a word of it—

LAUREY

You'll find out some day—

AUNT ELLER

Onct when you was a little girl you know what you done? Looked outa the winder and seen a cow standin' in the tool shed, and you said to yer Maw, "I knowed it, I knowed it! I knowed the cow ud eat the grindstone up!" Didn't you? But the cow didn't, though!

LAUREY (*smiling with great relief*)

No, the cow didn't.

AUNT ELLER

Well, then! You didn't know's much's you thought

you did. (*She goes and looks out the window.*) Now who'd you reckon that is drove up? (*A dog begins barking angrily.*) Why, it's that ole pedler! The one that sold me that egg-beater. Jist let me git my hands onto him—'f I don't fix him—!
[*She rushes toward the door.*

LAUREY

He's got someone with him. Why, it's Ado Annie Carnes! Now ain't she a sight! Ridin' around with that ole pedler.

AUNT ELLER

I'll th'ow him in the branch, that's whut I'll do to him! You know whut he done? Told me that egg-beater ud beat up eggs, and wring out dish rags, and turn the ice cream freezer, and I don't know whut all!—
[*She dashes out the door.*

LAUREY (*leaning out the window*)

Yoohoo! Ado Annie! C'm here. And bring yer pedler man in too, 'f you ain't afeard I'll take him away from you. (*She snickers with delight.*) I want to buy some things.
[*She flies to the dresser, catches up her hair in the back, straightens her dress, and by the time* ADO ANNIE CARNES *appears in the door is humming softly to herself, apparently having forgotten her uneasiness of the moment before.*

ADO ANNIE (*coming in*)
Hi.

[*She is an unattractive, stupid-looking farm girl,
with taffy-colored hair pulled back from a freckled
face. Her dress is of red gingham, and very unbe-
coming.*

LAUREY

Hi, yerself. Ridin' a piece?

ADO ANNIE (*non-committally*)

Rode over yere.

LAUREY

Well, set. Whur's yer pedler?

ADO ANNIE (*hiding a grin*)

Aw, he ain't *mine*. He's out there fightin' with Aunt
Eller 'bout that ole egg-beater.

LAUREY (*teasing her*)

Now listen here, have you tuck up with a pedler that
ud sell a pore old womern a egg-beater that wasn't
no good? Ado Annie Carnes, I'm plum ashamed of
you! You ort to be strapped.

ADO ANNIE

Ain't tuck up with him. Rode a piece in his ole buggy
for I was comin' over here, anyway, to ast about—to
ast you sump'n.

LAUREY

Whut was you gonna ast me, then?

ADO ANNIE

'F you was goin' to that there party over to Peck's.

LAUREY

Course I am.

ADO ANNIE

Well.

LAUREY

Don't I go to all the parties?

ADO ANNIE

I guess. You got fellers, lots of fellers.

LAUREY

Three hundred and fifty.

ADO ANNIE

Oh, you ain't!

LAUREY

Oh, I have.

ADO ANNIE

I kinda wondered 'f you wouldn't take *me*.

LAUREY

Me, take *you?*
[*She becomes strange and thoughtful.*

ADO ANNIE

Well, someone's takin' you, ain't they? You could take me along.

LAUREY

Why, my goodness! (*She beams ecstatically.*) Why, I'd jist love to have you, Ado Annie! You git yerself

over here to supper all diked up and fancy, and I'll
see that you got a way to go, all right. I'll put myself out!—(*She has another brilliant idea, which
amuses her very much.*) Oh, and I'm gonna buy you
sump'n so purty the fellers'll all fall over a wagon
tongue a-lookin' at you! Whur *is* that man! (*She
rushes to the door, in a fever of delight.*) Aunt Eller,
Aunt Eller! Quit a-botherin' that man from his
business! I want to buy some of his dewdads. (*To*
ADO ANNIE, *with mock gravity.*) You don't want to
git to like a pedler man *too* good, Ado Annie. You
hear me? They got wives in ever' state in the union.

ADO ANNIE

Oh, foot!

LAUREY

They have! And other places besides. Why, Alaska's
jist full of women a-livin' in ice-houses, and freezin'
to death 'cause of pedlers runnin' off and leavin' 'em
'thout no kindlin' er nuthin'—

ADO ANNIE

Aw!

LAUREY

A man *told* me! Shore as shootin'! He knowed a
Eskimo womern that a pedler up there went off and
left, and she had to sell her hair—a hundred hairs
at a time—jist cut it right off—to keep from
starvin' to death. Finally, she looked like a ole shave
head, bald-headed as a turkey buzzard, and she tuck
cold and died.

ADO ANNIE

Who did?

LAUREY

The *womern!*

ADO ANNIE

My goodness!
[AUNT ELLER *and the* PEDLER *come in. He is a little wiry, swarthy Syrian, neatly dressed, and with a red bandanna around his neck. He is very acquisitive, very cunning. He sets down his bulging suitcases, his little beady eyes sparkling professionally. He rushes over and, to* LAUREY's *alarm, kisses her hand.*

PEDLER

My, oh, my! But you are grown lady, Miss Laurey!
[*He gives a grunt of surprised pleasure. His speech is some blurred European tongue with Middle Western variations, from dealing almost entirely with farmers.*

LAUREY (*backing away*)

Heavens and earth!

PEDLER

Growed up, and sich a be-*youty*, too! My, oh my! I don't see you in a whole year. Last time you was little, like that, all sunburnt and bony, and now you've turned into a be-*you*tiful young lady. Yum, yum!
[*He kisses her hand again.*

LAUREY

Quit it, a-bitin' me! 'F you ain't had no breakfast go and eat yerself a green apple. Lands a goodness! You'd think I was angel food cake er sump'n.
[*But she is a little pleased, in spite of herself.*

PEDLER

Angel cake, that's jist whut you air! Angel cake, and jist hot outa the oven!

LAUREY

My, listen at him! Shet up yer mouth, and show me sump'n. Is that the way he talks to you, Ado Annie?

ADO ANNIE

Aw, he don't talk to me!

LAUREY

Mercy, whut does he *do* to you!

PEDLER

Now Aunt Eller, jist listen at the way she does me—

AUNT ELLER (*snapping at him*)

I aint yer *Aunt Eller!* Don't you *call* me Aunt Eller, you little wart! I'm mad at you.

PEDLER

Don't you go and be mad with me. Tell you what. I'll give you sump'n—give you another egg-beater.

AUNT ELLER

Don't you go and say *egg-beater* to me *again!*

PEDLER

Well, I'll give you sump'n—sump'n purty.

AUNT ELLER

Whut'll it be, and it'd better be good?

PEDLER

You wait. Sump'n purty for to wear.

AUNT ELLER (*snorting*)

Foot! I got things for to wear. Wouldn't have it. Whur is it?

PEDLER

You wait. I'll show you.

AUNT ELLER

Biggest liar I ever knowed! You'll be tellin' me next you got it hid some'eres, tied onto the horse's belly band—

PEDLER

That's whur it is, exactly! You guessed it!

AUNT ELLER

Lands, you big—I won't listen at you, won't stay in the same room whur you're at. (*She marches out of the room and slams the door. Then she opens it and comes back in.*) Thought I was gone, didn't you? Well, I ain't. I'm gonna stay right here, fer spite. Not gonna leave you and two girls in no bedroom, all by yerselves.

[*She sits down, in the corner.*

LAUREY (*in a kind of abstracted ecstasy*)

Want some hair-pins, a fine-tooth comb, a pink un. Want a buckle made out of shiny silver to fasten

onto my shoes! Want a dress with lace! Want pe'-
fume, face whitenin'! Wanta be purty, wanta smell
like a honeysuckle vine!

AUNT ELLER (*from her corner*)

Give her a cake of soap.

LAUREY (*her mood rising*)

Want things I c'n see and put my hands on. Want
things I've heared of and never had before—pearls
in a plush box, diamonds, a rubber-t'ard buggy, a
cut glass sugar bowl. Want things I caint tell you
about. Caint see 'em clear. Things nobody ever heared
of. (*Passionately, in a low voice.*) Not only things
to look at and hold in yer hands. Things to *happen*
to you! Things so nice if they ever did happen yer
heart ud quit beatin', you'd fall down dead. They
ain't no end to the things I want. Everything you
got wouldn't be a starter fer me, Mister Pedler Man!
(*Breaking off.*) So jist give me a bottle of shoe
blackin', and make it quick!

PEDLER (*on his knees, at his suitcases, handing them
out*)

Some nice garters? Silk in 'em, real silk, too, and
bows on 'em! Look at 'em. Made in Persia. Brought
to this country—

AUNT ELLER (*satirically*)

Brought to this country at great riskin' of life and
limb—like them Monsters from Madagascar. (*She
giggles.*) Lemme look at 'em.

LAUREY (*taking them*)

Jist whut I was a-wantin'—

PEDLER

Try 'em on.

LAUREY

Fer Ado Annie.

ADO ANNIE (*overcome*)

Aw!

PEDLER

Four bits apiece.

LAUREY

Four bits a pair.

PEDLER

Apiece.

LAUREY

Keep 'em, then.

PEDLER

Oh, take 'em.

LAUREY (*taking them*)

Here, Ado Annie. Put 'em on when no one ain't a-lookin'. (*To the* PEDLER.) You got any face whitenin'?

PEDLER (*finding it*)

The best they is, Miss Laurey. Liquid powder. Smells like the Queen of Egyp'! Put it on you, they cain't no one stay away from you. Reg'ler love drops! And only six bits a bottle—with a sponge throwed in.

LAUREY

Lemme see it. C'm here, Ado Annie. (*She puts* ADO
ANNIE *in a chair.*) Now be still, I'm gonna try it on
you. Now don't scrooge around like you had a ring
worm or sump'n. Gonna hide them freckles 'f I have
to put it on a inch thick.

[*She begins putting the liquid powder on a sponge
and dabbing at* ADO ANNIE's *face.* AUNT ELLER *leans
back in her chair and begins to sing, in derision.*

AUNT ELLER (*singing*)

Young men they'll go courting, they'll dress up so
    fine,
To cheat the poor girls is all their design,
They'll hug and they'll kiss and they'll cheat and
    they'll lie,
They'll keep the girls up till they're ready to die.
    Sing down, hidery down!

Those girls will get angry, they'll rise up and
    say:
"I am so sleepy, I wish you'd go 'way."
Those boys will get angry to hear the girls' scorn—
Before they'll go home, they'll sleep in some barn.
    Sing down, hidery down!

Oh, early next morning those laddies will rise,
Brush off the straws and rub up their eyes,
They'll saddle their horses and away they will ride
Like all true lovers dressed up in their pride.
    Sing down, hidery down!

Let us turn from those boys and turn from those lads
And turn to those girls which are twice as bad.
They'll flour up their faces and comb up their hair
Till they look like an owl in the bresh, I'll declare!
    Wo, larry, wo!

It's two long hours they'll stand at the glass,
And a thousand pins it will take them to dress,
They'll dress up so neat, and vanish away,
The devil himself couldn't look half so gay.
    Wo, larry, wo!

You can tell a good girl wherever she goes—
No foolish marks about her clothes,
No ribbons or rings or any such things,
But an old straw bonnet tied under her chin.
    Wo, larry, wo!

Of all the good lives 'tis bachelor's best.
Be drunk or be sober, lie down and take rest,
No wife to scold, no children to squall—
How happy's the man that keeps bachelor's hall.
    Wo, larry, wo!

(*She gets up from her chair to see what* LAUREY *is
doing.*) Let's see whut you're a-doin' to her. (*She
turns* ADO ANNIE *about in her chair, and bursts into
a loud guffaw.* ADO ANNIE'S *face is plastered with
white.*) Mercy! She's plum whitewashed you! Look
like a nigger angel turned all white and shinin'.
Whur's yer wings at, Angel?

ADO ANNIE (*scrubbing at her face*)

I'll take ever' bit of it off! Won't have no sich of a mess on me. I'm goin' right home! You've made a plumb sight outa me!
[*She makes for the door, flustered to death.*

LAUREY (*holding on to her*)

Don't you b'lieve her, Ado Annie! Why, you look purty as one of them rider ladies in the circus—'cept fer not havin' on no pink tights. Well, jist look in the lookin' glass, you don't b'lieve me.
[*There is a muffled pistol shot somewhere outside. They all start violently.*

AUNT ELLER

Now, whut in the name of—

PEDLER

Shootin'—

ADO ANNIE

I'm goin' home—

LAUREY (*her face white*)

Wait a minute! Whur was that shot, Aunt Eller? It wasn't out there—out there—?

AUNT ELLER

Sounded like it come from the smoke-house—

LAUREY

Don't you say it! It couldn't be, couldn't!

AUNT ELLER

It *was*, I tell you.
[*There is another shot.*

LAUREY (*shaken with fear*)

Curly!

AUNT ELLER (*looking at her in alarm*)

Why, you're 's white as a sheet, Laurey!

LAUREY (*rushing toward the door*)

Why'd you let him go out there whur Jeeter is!

AUNT ELLER

It couldn't be nuthin', honey!

LAUREY

We got to go see!
[*She hurries out the door,* AUNT ELLER *and the* PED-
LER *following.* ADO ANNIE *takes out her garters, puts
them on hastily, and flies out after them.*

CURTAIN

SCENE THREE

*It is immediately after Scene One—at the same time
as Scene Two.*

*The smoke-house is a dark, dirty building where the
meat was once kept. But now, the floor is full of holes;
at night the field mice scurry about the room. The rafters are worn and decayed, smoky, covered with dust
and cobwebs. On a low loft, many things are stored—
horse-collars, plowshares, bridles, jars of fruit, a saddle, binder twine, a keg of nails. Under it, the four-
poster bed is grimy and never made. A pair of muddy
shoes and a pair of gum boots are lying on their sides
under the bed. On the walls, of unpainted two-by-
twelves, soiled clothes are hanging, also tobacco ad-
vertisements, an enlisting poster, a pink cover off the
Police Gazette, a large framed picture of Dan Patch,
several postcard pictures of teams pulling heavy loads
of logs, etc. In one corner, there are hoes, rakes and an
axe. In another, a bale of hay covered with a red saddle blanket. In the room also, a tool box, several rough
chairs, a table, a spittoon, a wash-stand, several farm
lanterns, a rope, a mirror for shaving. A small window
lets in a little light, but not much. The door at back is
closed.*

JEETER *sits in a low chair looking at some postcards,
leaning forward now and then to spit at the spittoon.
He is about thirty-five, with a curious earth-colored*

face and hairy hands. He wears heavy brogans, a greasy pair of trousers, two shirts open at the neck, and both dirty. He is always absorbed, dark, and sullen. Hearing a knock, he shifts about in his chair, spits again, shoves the pictures quickly back into his pocket, and says crossly:

JEETER

Well, cain't you open it?
[CURLY *opens the door and comes in.*

CURLY

Howdy—

JEETER (*unpleasantly*)

Is that yore plug tied to that peach tree?

CURLY

'F you mean that horse, that's my horse. He ain't no plug.

JEETER

Plug or no plug, you mighta tied him some'eres else.

CURLY

They ain't nary a peach on that tree.

JEETER

And they *won't* be, if everbody's gonna tie his saddle horse to it.

CURLY

I'll go and move him.

JEETER

'S too late, pardner. I done moved him.

CURLY

Whur'd you put him at?

JEETER

Turned him a-loose.

CURLY (*unruffled*)

That's all right.

JEETER

He's prob'ly tuck off up the road by this time, and serve you right.

CURLY

Left the reins a-draggin', didn't you?

JEETER

Yes, I did.

CURLY

Well, that's a cow pony, that is. He'll stand all day if the reins is down.

JEETER (*disappointed*)

You orten't to go around a-tyin' him to peach trees.

CURLY

You know, I don't know a peach tree from a corn stalk.

JEETER

Better learn, then. Whut'd you want around here, anyhow?

CURLY

I done got th'ough my business—up here at the house. I jist thought I'd come in and see you.

JEETER

I ain't got time to see no one. I'm a-takin' a bath.

CURLY (*facetiously*)

Thought you was balin' hay.

JEETER

How's that?

CURLY

I say, that's a good-lookin' rope you got there. (*He points.*) Buy it at Claremore?

JEETER

Cain't see that that's none of *yore* business.

CURLY

I know you didn't steal it.

JEETER (*shortly*)

That rope was *give* to me. It's a used un.

CURLY

Ort to spin, then. (*He goes over, takes it down and begins spinning it.*) You know Will Parker?

JEETER

Never heared of him.

CURLY

Ole man Parker's boy up here by Claremore? He can shore spin a rope. Chews gum when he spins it. Gum ain't healthy, I always say. (*Holding on to one end of the rope, he tosses the other over a rafter, and catches it. He pulls down on both ends, tentatively.*)

'S a good strong rafter you got there. You could hang yerself on that, Jeeter.

JEETER

I could—what?

CURLY (*cheerfully*)

Hang yerself. It ud be easy as fallin' off a log! Fact is, you could stand on a log—er a cheer if you'd ruther—right about here, see, and put this here around yer neck. Tie that good up there first, of course. Then, all you'd have to do would be to fall off the log—er the cheer, whichever you'd ruther fall off of. In five minutes, er less, with good luck, you'd be dead as a door nail.

JEETER (*suspiciously*)

Whut'd you mean by that?

CURLY

The folks ud all gether around and sing. *Sad* songs, of course. And some of 'em ud say whut a good man you was, and others ud say what a pig-stealer and a hound dog you was, and you'd orter been in the penitentiary long ago, fer orneriness.

JEETER

You better be keerful, now!

CURLY

I ain't sayin' it. I'm sayin' *they'd* say it. You know the way people talks—like a swarm of mud wasps. (*Looking about the room.*) So this is whur *you* live?

Always like to see whur a man's a-livin' at. You got
a fine place here, Mr. Jeeter. Matches you.
[*He grins mischievously.* JEETER *gets up, goes over
close to him, dangerously.*

JEETER

I don't know who you air er nuthin'—but I think
you'd better tell me whut you come bustin' in here
fer, makin' free 'th my things and talkin' the way
you talk.

CURLY

Why, my name's Curly. Thought you knowed. Curly
McClain. Born on a farm in Kansas. Cowpuncher by
trade and by profession. I break broncs, mean uns.
I bull-dog steers. I ain't never been licked, and I
ain't never been shot. Shot *at*, but not *shot*. I got
a good disposition, too, and when anything seems
like to me it's funny, why I let loose and laugh till
my belt breaks in two and my socks falls down. Whut
on earth air *you* doin' 'th a pitcher of Dan Patch?
[*He points to the picture.*

JEETER (*nonplussed*)
Got a right to have a pitcher of Dan Patch, ain't I?

CURLY
Yeah, and you shore have. And that there pink
pitcher there, now that's a naked womern, ain't it?

JEETER
Yer eyes don't lie to you.

CURLY

Plumb stark naked as a jaybird! No. No, she ain't, not *quite*. Got a couple of thingumabobs tied on to her.

JEETER

That's a cover off the Police Gazette.

CURLY

Wouldn't do fer me to have sich a pitcher around.

JEETER

Whut's wrong with it?

CURLY

I never seen sich a pitcher! That ud give me idys, that would!

JEETER (*at home now and at ease with his guest*)

Shucks, that ain't a thing to whut I got here!
[*He draws out his postcards.*

CURLY (*covering his eyes*)

I'll go blind! Whew! Lose my eyesight in a minute! I wonder now if we couldn't have a little game of pitch?

JEETER

Look at this here un. That's a dinger, that is!

CURLY (*looking at it gravely*)

Yeah, that shore *is* a dinger.

JEETER

The girls these is tuck of can shore make it inter-

estin' for a man! God, cain't they! Over at Tulsa. I
had me another whole pack of these—but I lost 'em—

CURLY

That's too bad. That was sump'n to lose.

JEETER

Yeah, stole off me over to a dance at Bushyhead.
Shore, I'll play a game of pitch with you, all right.
Here, set down.
[*They sit at the table.* JEETER *fishes in the drawer
and pulls out two pistols and a pack of dirty Bicycle
playing cards, and lays them on the table.*

CURLY

You—you got pistols, too?

JEETER

Good uns. Colt 45.

CURLY

Whut do you do 'th pistols?

JEETER

Shoot things.

CURLY

Oh. You deal.

JEETER

No, you deal.

CURLY

Shore, I'll deal. (*He shuffles the cards and begins to
deal.*) Is this draw?

JEETER

Suit yerself.

CURLY

Draw, then. With the Jick, and not the left Jack.
It's yore first bid.

JEETER

Two.

CURLY

Three.

JEETER

It's your'n.

CURLY

Spades. (*He takes up the deck again.*) How many?

JEETER

One.

[CURLY *deals one to* JEETER, *two to himself, picks up
his hand. They begin to play.*

CURLY (*with lyric warmth—for he is stating something
about his own life—and his feeling about life*)

Outside, the sun's jist crazy 'th the heat, beatin' on
the prairie and the corn stalks. Passed a field in the
bottom this mornin' whur the backwater had been.
Ground all cracked and blistered and bakin' in the
sun. Likin' it, though! Likin' it good. The crawfish
put up their pinchers and hustled about, 'cause their
holes is all goin' dry. Seen fields of wheat and oats—
fine as a fiddle! The crows went to honkin' at me

when I rode th'ough the Dog Crick timber, and I could see hundreds of squirrels friskin' in the blackjacks. I could smell them green walnuts, too, whenever old Dun ud tromp on 'em. Shore the purtiest mornin' in a long time! Felt like hollerin' and shoutin'. I raired away back in my saddle and ole Dun stepped out a-prancin' and we come th'ough Claremore like a streak of forked lightnin'! An' it's shore a funny end to a fine purty mornin' to find yerself shet up in a dark hole bent over a table a-fingerin' a pack of cards 's greasy 's a ole tin spoon, ain't it? Yeah, that's the way it is, though, in this here life. Got to git used to it. (*He begins to sing.*)

Oh, my name it is Sam Hall, it is Sam Hall,
My name it is Sam Hall, it is Sam Hall,
My name it is Sam Hall, and I hate you one and all,
I hate you one and all, damn yer eyes!

To the gallows I must go, I must go,
To the gallows I must go, I must go,
To the gallows I must go, for I've killed a man you
    know,
Because he loved her so, damn his eyes!

I must hang till I am dead, I am dead,
I must hang till I am dead, I am dead,
I must hang till I am dead, for I killed a man, they
    said,
And I left him there for dead, damn his eyes!

I saw Mollie in the crowd, in the crowd,
I saw Mollie in the crowd, in the crowd,

I saw Mollie in the crowd, and I hollered right out
loud:

"Hey, Mollie, ain't you proud, damn yer eyes!"

[*As he sings the game goes slower and slower*, CURLY
interested in the song and in JEETER, JEETER *frowning and strangely excited. Suddenly a dog begins
barking angrily.* JEETER *goes to the door quickly
and looks out.*

JEETER

Who would that be, I wonder? In a buggy. Got a girl
with him. Oh! (*He is relieved.*) It's that Syrian pedler. Yeah, that's who. (*He closes the door and comes
down again. After a moment.*) Did that—did that
Sam Hall kill the feller? (CURLY *nods.*) He'd orta
killed the girl, too.

CURLY

They wouldn't a-been much fun in that.

JEETER

Fun! Whut was fun about it, anyway! (*Strangely,
darkly, his tongue unloosed.*) I knowed a feller onct
killed a girl. He'd been keepin' comp'ny with her and
aimed to marry her. One day he found her up in the
barn loft with another man. He didn't do nuthin' at
first. But this girl lived on a farm with her folks.
One night her paw and maw couldn't sleep fer the
dog a-barkin' so. Next mornin' the old man went
down to feed the stock like he always did, and when
he come to the horse troft, he seen sump'n white
a-layin' there. It was his daughter, in her nightgown,

layin' there in the water all covered with blood, dead. They never did find out who done it. But I met up with a man onct on the road-gang a-makin' that road from here to Collinsville, and he told me he done it. Only—you know what he done? Made out this murder tuck place ten year ago back in Missouri. It didn't, though! It was up here by Sweetwater not two year ago—and I'd saw all about it in the paper! But I didn't let on. Whut a liar he was!

CURLY

And a kind of a—a kind of a murderer, too, wasn't he?

JEETER (*absorbed*)

I couldn't make out why he cut her throat and then throwed her in the horse troft, too. Less'n—he thought—why, that's why! He'd got blood all over him, and he couldn't stand havin' blood on him, so that's why he done it! I knowed another case, too, of a man got a girl in trouble—

CURLY

I was jist goin' to ast you 'f you didn't know some other stories.

JEETER

This man was a married farmer, and he knowed this girl. It had been goin' on a long time till the man it looked like he couldn't live 'thout her. He was kinda crazy and wild if she'd even speak to anyone. One night, it was moonlight, and they'd met out back of an old mowin' machine left in the meader a-rustin'—

She told him about the way she was, gonna have a
baby. He went jist hog-wild, and found a piece of old
rope in the tool box of the mowin' machine, tied her
hands and feet with it, nen throwed her up on top of
a stack of hay, and set f'ar to it. Burned her to
death! Do you know why? He didn't keer about her
goin' to have the baby, that wasn't it. He jist didn't
know how he was goin' to live 'thout *havin'* her all the
time while she was carryin' it! So he killed her. Yeow,
it's funny the things people do, like that.

[CURLY *gets up, goes over, throws the door open. A
shaft of brilliant sunlight pours in, alive with mil-
lions of dust motes.*

CURLY

Git a little air in here. (*He goes back and sits down.*)
Yore mind seems to run on two things, don't it? Before you come here to work fer the Williams', whur
did you work?

JEETER (*hostile again*)

I don't know as that concerns no one but me.

CURLY

That's right, pardner. That's yore look-out.

JEETER

I'll tell you, though. Up by Quapaw. And before that
over by Tulsa. Bastards to work fer, both of 'em!

CURLY

Whut'd they do?

JEETER

Alwys makin' out they was *better*. Yeah, *lots* better!

Farmers they was, like me, wasn't they? Only not half as good.

CURLY

And whut'd you do—git even?

JEETER (*looks up at him, suspiciously*)

Who said anything about gittin' even?

CURLY

No one, that I recollect. It jist come in my head.

JEETER

Oh, it did? (*He gets up, goes over and shuts the door, turns in the gloom, comes and sits down again, and looks at* CURLY.) Whut was that business you had up here at the house?

CURLY (*after a moment*)

I don't know as that concerns you, does it?

JEETER

It does, though! If it's anything to do with this farm.

CURLY

I forgot you owned it.

JEETER

Never mind that! It couldn't be to buy hay, fer you got plenty of hay.

CURLY

How'd you know that?

JEETER

You work for Skidmore, don't you, tother side of Justus?

CURLY

Thought you didn't know me.

JEETER

I know you, all right. If he's sent you over to buy up the oat crop, why it's done spoke fer.

CURLY

Glad to find that out.

JEETER

We ain't got no cattle to sell, ner no cow ponies, you know that. And the farm ain't fer sale, and won't be.

CURLY

You shore relieved my mind considerable.

JEETER

They's only one thing left you could come snoopin' around here fer. And it ud better not be that!

CURLY (*easily*)

That's exactly whut it is!

JEETER (*white with anger*)

Better not be!

CURLY

It *is*, I tell you.

JEETER

I wouldn't come on the place if I was you! I wouldn't come here—

CURLY

Whut'll happen if I decide that's jist the right thing fer me to do?

JEETER

I'd git on my horse and go quick! Don't you come around that girl, you hear me?

CURLY (*scornfully*)

You shore got it bad. So you're takin' her to that party tonight? Jesus! She's got a taste. I don't know as it's worth fightin' about if she'd ruther go with you. I step out—cheerful as anything. You're welcome. (*Thoughtfully.*) Only—somebody ort to tell her whut you air. And fer that matter somebody ort to tell you onct about yerself.

JEETER

I've had jist about enough!

CURLY

If you'd like to do anything to me, now's the best chanct you'll ever have. (*Softly.*) You got two pistols, good uns, all loaded and ready to bark. They's a axe a-standin' in the corner. A bright bright sickle, right off the grindstone hangs over there on a nail and shines. Yer hoes is sharp, yer razor's got two edges onto it, and nary a one of 'em is rusty. And it ain't very light in here, is it? Not half light enough. A feller wouldn't feel very safe in here 'th you, 'f he didn't know you. (*Acidly.*) But I *know* you, Jeeter. I've knowed you fer a long time.

JEETER (*half rising*)

You don't know a thing about me—

CURLY

The country's full of people like you! I been around.

(*His voice rises dramatically.*) In this country, they's two things you c'n do if you're a man. Live out of doors is one. Live in a hole is the other. I've set by my horse in the bresh some'eres and heared a rattlesnake many a time. Rattle, rattle, rattle!— he'd go, skeered to death. Skeered—and *dangerous!* Somebody comin' close to his hole! Somebody gonna step on him! Git his old fangs ready, full of pizen! Curl up and wait! Fer as long's you live in a hole, you're skeered, you got to have pertection. You c'n have muscles, oh, like arn—and still be as weak as a empty bladder—less'n you got things to barb yer hide with. (*Suddenly, harshly, directly to* JEETER.) How'd you git to be the way you air, anyway—settin' here in this filthy hole—and thinkin' the way you're thinkin'? Why don't you do sump'n healthy onct in a while, 'stid of stayin' shet up here a-crawlin' and festerin'!

JEETER

Shet up, you!

CURLY

You'll die of yer own pizen, I tell you!

JEETER

Anh!
[*He seizes a gun in a kind of reflex, a kind of desperate frenzy, and pulls the trigger. The wall across the room is splintered by the shot.*

CURLY

Jesus! What was you shootin' at, Jeeter?

JEETER (*his hands on the two pistols, hoarsely*)

Never mind, now!

CURLY (*in a high excitement, but apparently cool and calm*)

You orta feel better now. Hard on the wall, though. I wish 't you'd let me show you sump'n. Jist reach me one of them pistols acrost here a minute— (JEETER *does not move, but sits staring into* CURLY'S *eyes.*) They's a knot-hole over there about as big as a dime. See it a-winkin'? I jist want to see if I c'n hit it. (*He leans over unhurriedly, with cat-like tension, picks up one of the pistols, turns in his chair, and fires at the wall high up. He turns in triumph.*) Didn't make a splinter! Bullet right through the knot-hole, 'thout tetchin', slick as a whistle, didn't I? I knowed I could do it. You saw it, too, didn't you? Somebody's comin', I 'spect. It's my play, ain't it?

[*He throws down a card.* JEETER *looks at the floor.* LAUREY, AUNT ELLER, *and the* PEDLER, *followed a moment later by* ADO ANNIE, *come running in at the door without knocking.*

AUNT ELLER (*gasping for breath*)

Whut's this? Who's been a-shootin'? Skeer the liver and lights out of a feller! Was that you, Curly? Don't set there, you lummy, answer when you're spoke to!

CURLY

Well, I shot onct.

AUNT ELLER

What was you shootin' at?

CURLY

See that knot-hole over there?

AUNT ELLER

I see lots of knot-holes.

CURLY

Well, it was one of them.

AUNT ELLER

Don't tell me you was shootin' at a knot-hole!

CURLY

I was, though.

AUNT ELLER (*exasperated*)

Well, ain't you a pair of purty nuthin's, settin' here
a-pickin' away at knot-holes 'th a pair of ole pistols
and skeerin' everybody to death! You've give that ole
turkey gobbler conniption fits. Ort to give you a good
Dutch rub and arn some of the craziness out of you!
Come 'ere, you all, they ain't nobody hurt. Jist a pair
of fools a-swappin' noises.

ADO ANNIE (*dumbly*)

Did someone shoot, Aunt Eller?

AUNT ELLER

Did someone *shoot!*

ADO ANNIE

Whut'd they shoot *at*, Aunt Eller?

AUNT ELLER

Yer grandmaw, silly!
[*She goes out.*

ADO ANNIE

My lands!
[*She follows her out.* LAUREY *and the* PEDLER *stand in the door.*

LAUREY (*after a moment*)

Curly.

CURLY

Yeah.

LAUREY

Did you *hit* that knot-hole?

CURLY

How's that?

LAUREY

I say, did you *hit* that knot-hole?

CURLY (*puzzled*)

Yeah, I—I hit it.

LAUREY (*cryptically*)

Well. That was good, wasn't it?
[*She goes out, smiling. The* PEDLER *bounds into life and comes forward with great animation.*

PEDLER

Well, well. Mr. Jeeter! Don't trouble yerself. Fine day, and a good crop comin'. You too, Mr. Curly. (*Lowering his voice.*) Now then, we're all by our-selves, I got a few little purties, private knick-knacks for to show you. Special for the men folks. (*He winks*

*mysteriously, and draws out of his inside coat pocket
a thin flat box and opens it out on the table.*) Yes
sir, special. The things you cain't get and 've got
to have. All them little things a man needs in his
business, eh? (*He points.*) Jist look at them things.
Agin the law, ever one of 'em! There's brass knucks,
lay a man out jist like he was dead in one good hard
hit. Fit any knuckle and break any head. And—in
the little package, well, I won't tell you!— Jist open
her up, and you'll see— The little dinguses that you
got to have. Fancy! Lots of colors and jiggers onto
'em. French! Yes, sir! French—right out of Paris.
And jackknives and frog-stickers. Steel and never
rusty. Kill a hog or a bastard eh, it's all the same to
them little ones! And postcards! Kansas City Best.
Made right. Take 'em away, they're hard on the
eyes! And here's dice, playing cards. Everything you
need, everything a man could want. Look 'em over
and if they's any little thing you need, jist point,
jist make the signs, and I'm right here— Now then,
how's that?

JEETER (*rousing himself*)

How much is that frog-sticker?

PEDLER (*taking out a long wicked-looking knife and
opening it*)

That frog-sticker. That's reasonable, reasonable. I
won't charge you much for a knife like that. 'F you
got it in Claremore, you know whut you pay? Twice
my price, jist twice. 'F you could get it. That's a
good frog-sticker, that is, and I'm sellin' it cheap

to you, Mr. Jeeter—fer a man hadn't ort to be *without* a good frog-sticker, it ain't safe, he might need it. He never knows why and he never knows when. Don't see nuthin' to interest you, Mr. Curly?

CURLY (*slowly*)

I was jist thinkin' myself—that mebbe—jist fer the looks of the thing—and to kinda have it around—I might consider—buyin'—if they're good and not too high—and can be depended on—a nice hard pair of them brass knucks you got there—
[*He reaches over and picks them up.*

CURTAIN

SCENE FOUR

Lead her up and down the little brass wagon,
Lead her up and down the little brass wagon,
Lead her up and down the little brass wagon,
For she's the one, my darling!

One wheel off and the axle draggin',
One wheel off and the axle draggin',
One wheel off and the axle draggin',
For she's the one, my darling!

Spokes all broke and the tongue a-waggin',
Spokes all broke and the tongue a-waggin',
Spokes all broke and the tongue a-waggin',
For she's the one, my darling!

Blistered brakes and sides all saggin',
Blistered brakes and sides all saggin',
Blistered brakes and sides all saggin',
For she's the one, my darling!

The party is in full swing in the back yard of OLD MAN
PECK's *place across Dog Creek. There are a few benches
on the porch and a large coalstove. A primitive, rough-
hewn built-in cabinet runs along one end of the porch
and on it are piled all manner of miscellaneous things—
ropes, cans of nails, a vinegar bottle, sacks of salt and
sugar, home-dried apricots and peaches, a guitar, a*

*fiddle, jars of home-made preserves. On the walls are
hanging strings of popcorn on the cob, red peppers,
onions hanging by their tops, the dried pelt of a possum,
etc. Kerosene lanterns hung to the wall light up the
yard. Light streams out from the house. Around the
corner of the house can be seen the stone well with its
wide arch of iron and its pulley, a tremendous walnut
tree and the night sky.*

*The farm boys and the cowboys have forgotten their
corn plowing, their day in the hay field, their day on
the range. They have put up the mules, doused themselves at the pump, bolted a supper of fried salt pork,
potatoes and gravy and hot biscuits, and now in their
store clothes and their chaps and their overalls they
grin and sweat and stomp, their voices loud and harsh
in the singing. Those who are not playing at the moment lounge in the doorway, chewing tobacco and smok-
ing; some have gone out behind the barn or to their
buggies and saddle pockets for a shot of liquor.*

*Most of the girls are dressed in white and wear bright
bows. Some have tiny watches pinned to their dresses,
and carry handkerchiefs.* OLD MAN PECK *is clapping his
hands. He is an old timer, grizzled and genial, about sev-
enty. He has gone to play-parties and dances now for
fifty years, and knows every trick, every extra stomp,
every variation in the songs, every sly elaboration of the
do si do.*

*The voices crack on the high notes, the feet pound,
hands clap, the jars on the high cabinet rattle, dust
clouds the air. "The Little Brass Wagon" ends in a
burst of high, excited, exhausted laughter. Immediately,
on a peak of gaiety, hardly stopping to mop their brows,*

the men begin getting partners for a square dance, call-
ing loudly, grabbing the girls carelessly around the
waist and getting slapped for their temerity.

OLD MAN PECK (*leaping out into the middle of the floor*
and holding up his hands)

Hey! Boys and gals! Git in the kitchen fer the candy
pullin'.
[*The crowd breaks, and dashes in the house noisily.*
OLD MAN PECK *is about to follow.*

AUNT ELLER (*calling from the darkness off left*)

Lands sake, I'm all tangled up in it. Curly, help me,
cain't you?

CURLY (*off*)

Well, be still, quit a-buckin' up.

AUNT ELLER

Mr. Peck! Mr. Peck, you ole fool, come an' help a
lady, cain't you!

OLD MAN PECK

Is that you, Aunt Eller? Whut's the matter?

AUNT ELLER (*entering with* CURLY)

Matter! Say, do you have to have barbed w'ar layin'
around all over the yard? Gettin' me all tangled up in
it! 'F it hadn't a-been fer *me* I'd a-lost a leg. Whur's
Mary?

OLD MAN PECK

Oh, I got the ole womern out in the smoke-house.

AUNT ELLER

Doin' all the work, I bet.

OLD MAN PECK

Yep, that's right. You're kinda late, ain't you?

AUNT ELLER

Got here quick 's I could make it. Say, is this whur the party's at—out here in the yard?

OLD MAN PECK

It's too hot in the house.

AUNT ELLER

Well, it's kinda purty out here, I must say. Here— hang this up.

OLD MAN PECK (*taking the lamp she holds out*)

Whur'd you get that?

AUNT ELLER (*grinning*)

Pulled it off the dashboard. Guess I'll go in and take off my fascinator. (*Taking* CURLY *by the arm.*) How'd you like my feller I went and ketched?

CURLY (*smiling, and taking her by the arm*)

How'd you like my girl I went and ketched?

OLD MAN PECK

Both of you is all right, I reckon. Whur's Laurey at?

CURLY (*pausing as he realizes what this means*)

Laurey, ain't she here yit?

OLD MAN PECK

Course not. Thought you was gonna bring her.

CURLY (*concerned*)

They ort to be here, Aunt Eller. Whutta you reckon's

happened? They started 'fore we did—half a hour before.

AUNT ELLER (*quieting him*)

Aw, they're jist poky. They're drivin' Old Eighty, and that fool mare is alwys wantin' to graze 'long side the road. Now don't look so worried, Curly, they'll git here. Come on in, and le's see *who's* come with *who*.

[*They go in. A burst of greeting floats out.*

SHORTY (*a cowboy, staggers in, drunk*)

Say, Mr. Peck, is that yore big old white cow standin' out there by the grainary?

OLD MAN PECK

Hi, Shorty. Yeah, she's mine. Give two gallon and a half a day.

SHORTY

Whew, she like to skeered me to death. Thought she was a ghost—till she said *Moo.*

OLD MAN PECK

You must be drinkin' a little, Shorty.

SHORTY (*speaking as he makes for the door*)

Me? I ain't drinkin'. I'm drunk.

[*He goes into the house.*

OLD MAN PECK (*spying* JEETER, ADO ANNIE *and* LAUREY. JEETER *is carrying a lighted lantern which he hangs up*)

Oh, *here* you air. We been wonderin' whur you was.

ADO ANNIE *and* LAUREY

Hi, Mr. Peck.

OLD MAN PECK

Most everbody's here that's comin', I 'spect. I got to go out to the smoke-house, and see about the ice cream freezin'. Go on in, and git yer pardners for the next set.

[*He disappears around the corner of the house* LAUREY *starts in the house.*

JEETER (*stopping her*)

I wanta see you.

LAUREY (*a little frightened*)

Well, here I am, so look yer eyes full.

JEETER

Ado Annie, go inside.

LAUREY (*grabbing her*)

Ado Annie, you stay here a minute.

ADO ANNIE (*pulling loose*)

Shoot! I wanta see 'f I cain't git me a pardner, 'fore they're all gone.

[*She dashes in.*

JEETER

Whut'd you ast that Ado Annie to ride with us fer?

LAUREY

She didn't have no way to go.

JEETER

That ain't yore lookout. Why don't you wanta be
with me by yerself?

LAUREY

Why, I don't know whut you're talkin' about! I'm
with you by myself now, ain't I?

JEETER

You wouldn't a-been, you coulda got out of it.

LAUREY (*impatiently*)

Well, now 'at I *am*, whut'd you want?

JEETER

Nuthin'—but—

LAUREY

Well, fer land's-a-livin'! (*She makes for the door.*)
Of all the crazies!

JEETER (*getting in front of the door*)

Mornin's you stay hid in yer room all the time.
Nights you set in the front room and won't git outa
Aunt Eller's sight— (*In a strange hoarse excitement.*) Ain't saw you by yerself in a long time! Why
ain't I? First time was last year's thrashin'. You
was watchin' the chaff fly and them knives a-cloppin'
at the bundles. I come around the corner of the stack
and you stood there a-wavin' yer sunbonnet to keep
some of the dust offen you, and you said to me to
git you a drink of water. I *got* you a drink of water.
I brung the jug around. I give it to you. I *did* give
it to you, didn't I?

LAUREY (*frightened*)

I don't know whut you mean.

JEETER (*as before*)

Last time it was winter 'th snow six inches deep in drifts when I was sick. You brung me that hot soup out to the smoke-house and give it to me, and me in bed. I hadn't shaved in two weeks. You ast me 'f I had any fever and you put yer hand on my head to see. Why'd you do that? Whut'd you tetch me for! (*He suddenly seizes her in his arms, his voice thick with excitement.*) You won't git away from me—!

LAUREY (*trying to free herself*)

You better le' me alone!

JEETER

You've kep' outa my way, and kep' outa my way—

LAUREY

Quit it, quit it—!

JEETER

Cain't think of nuthin' else! It's killin' me. Lay awake at nights. God damn you, quit a-tryin' to git away— I got you now—
[*He holds her closer.*

LAUREY (*in revulsion*)

Oh!
[*She turns her head aside, frightened and shaken.*

JEETER

So goddamned purty!

[*She frees an arm and strikes him in the face, with desperate strength. He releases her, and stands uncomprehending, tranced. She backs away, watching him.*

LAUREY (*almost hysterically*)

Now le' me go, le' me outa here 'fore I holler and tell on you!

JEETER (*after a moment, slowly*)

You hit me— (*Breaking out, violently.*) Like 'em all! I ain't good enough, am I? I'm a h'ard hand, ain't I? Got dirt on my hands, pig slop— Ain't fitten to tetch you! You're better, so goddamned much better! Yeah, we'll see who's better—we'll see who's better, Miss Laurey! Nen you'll wish 't you wasn't so free 'th yer airs, you're sich a fine lady—!

LAUREY (*suddenly so angry, all her fear vanishes*)

Air you makin' threats—to *me?* Air you standin' there tryin' to tell me 'f I don't 'low you to slobber over me like a hog, why you're gonna do sump'n about it! Why, you're a mangy dog and somebody'd orta shoot you! (*With enormous scorn.*) Yeah, I ort to 'low you yer own way, I reckon. Sich a great, big, fine strappin' man so full of dazzle I ort to git down on my knees to him! Christ all hemlock! (*Sharply, her eyes blazing.*) You think so much about bein' h'ard hand. Well, I'll jist tell you sump'n that'll rest yer brain, Mr. Jeeter! You ain't a h'ard hand fer me, no more! You c'n jist pack up yer duds and scoot! Oh, and I even got better idys 'n that! You ain't to come on the place again, you hear me? I'll send yer stuff any place you say, but don't you 's much 's set foot inside the pasture gate or I'll sic the dogs onto you! Now then, next time you go makin' threats to people, you better think a few thinks first and spit on yer hands fer good luck!

JEETER (*standing quite still, absorbed, dark, his voice low*)

Said yer say. Brought it on yerself. (*In a voice harsh with an inner frenzy.*) Cain't he'p it, I tell you! Sump'n brung it on you. On me, too. Cain't never rest. Cain't be easy. That's the way it is. Ay, I told you the way it was! You wouldn't listen—

[*He goes out, passes the corner of the house and disappears.* LAUREY *stands a moment, held by his strangeness, then she starts toward the house, changes her mind and sinks onto a bench, a frightened little girl again.* ADO ANNIE *bounds out of the house, excited. She sees* LAUREY.

ADO ANNIE (*worried*)

Laurey, I got sump'n to tell you.

LAUREY (*standing up quickly*)

Ado Annie, is Curly in there?

ADO ANNIE

Yes he's in there, but . . . Laurey, now look, Laurey, it's turrible—I gotta tell you—

LAUREY (*starting swiftly towards the house*)

Don't bother me.

ADO ANNIE (*catching at her*)

Now, Laurey, please, my lands, it's all yore fault, so you gotta tell me whut to do.

LAUREY

Well, whut is it?

ADO ANNIE

Them ole garters is s' tight they 'bout cut my laigs plum in two.

LAUREY

Well, take 'em off.

ADO ANNIE

Take 'em off? Have my stockings rollin' down onto my shoes? Wouldn't I be a purty sight?

LAUREY

You'd have all the boys a-runnin' after you right, you done that.

ADO ANNIE

You shore?

LAUREY

Shore, I'm shore.

ADO ANNIE

Aw, I wouldn't do it fer nuthin'.

LAUREY

Well I told you whut to do, you won't mind me.
[*She makes for the door.*

ADO ANNIE (*stopping her*)

Laurey! Them ole boys worries me. The minute I got in the house they started grabbin' at me. Whut'd they mean a-tellin' me, "Come out 'hind the barn 'th me?" That ole Payne boy said that.

LAUREY

Whyn't you ast him whut he meant?

ADO ANNIE

I was skeered he'd tell me.

LAUREY

Fiddlesticks! (*She starts again for the door, turns quickly, struck with an idea.*) Ado Annie, will you do sump'n fer me?

ADO ANNIE

'F it ain't too hard.

LAUREY

Go in there and find Curly, and tell him to come out here. I want to see him, I got to see him!
[*A man runs out of the house calling out* "Whee! Here's my girl! Come on here, Ado Annie, I'm goin' to swing you till you're dizzy as a loon!" *He whirls her around and around.* LAUREY, *distressed, starts for the house.*

A MAN (*coming out boisterously*)

Here, Laurey's *my* partner. Come on, Laurey, you promised me away back last August, purt' near.
[*He swings her into position for the next dance.*

OLD MAN PECK (*coming from the house*)
Git yore pardners like you done before,
Two big rings in the middle of the floor.
[*The others all sweep out, paired off and take their places for the square dance.*

CROWD (*falling into position*)
I hope there'll be a big fight!
Be lots of work for the shoemaker, tomorrow!
Watch yer honey, watch her close,
When you meet her, double the dose!
Eight hands up, and circle to the west!
[*They start to dance.*

OLD MAN PECK (*stopping them before they begin*)
Whoa, whoa, back, Maud! My, you're like a gang of mule colts! Quiet down, cain't you, they ain't no a-stoppin' you! Wanta tell you sump'n!

CROWD
Let 'er rip, grampaw!
Say yer say and git it outa you 'fore you choke on it!
Open up yer mouth and holler yer head off, see 'f I keer!

OLD MAN PECK
Now then, listen to me a minute! We gonna have a little singin' to give us a rest. You all 'll be so broke down in a minute you'll be blowin' like a thrashin' machine. Quiet down now, see 'f we cain't git somebody to sing sump'n— Time we sing a little bit, got a s'prise for you. You all know whur the smoke-house is, don't you?

CROWD

'Hind that ellum out there.

Shore, we know. Settin' on its foundations!

OLD MAN PECK

Well, I got the ole womern out there a-turnin' the
ice cream freezer, and a-makin' popcorn balls. And
jist as soon as we sing a little bit, everthing ort to
be ready. Er 'f it *ain't* ready, take a scantlin' to the
ole womern, I will, and blister her good! Now then,
who'll give us a song?

CROWD

Sing one yerself, Mr. Peck.

You ain't winded, air you?

Sing one of them ole ballets—

Sing "The Dyin' Cowboy." Oh, bury me not on the
lone prairee!

Sing that there un 'bout the blind child, while we
cry and take on, the pore little son of a gun, didn't
have no mammy!

OLD MAN PECK (*humorously*)

Aw, I'm bashful 's a blushin' bride! Anyways, all I
know is sad songs, make you cry. No, cain't I git
someone else—how 'bout you, Lizzie?

CROWD

The sadder the better!

Go on, you start things, git everbody limbered up—!

OLD MAN PECK

Tell you whut I'll do, then! Sing you "Custer's Last

Charge" an' 'f I ketch airy grin on any of you, gonna do sump'n, I'm tellin' you. And you better keep quiet and respectable-like, 'cause this yere is a serious piece.

CROWD

Go to it, Mr. Peck!
Serious 's a church.
Got my mouth sewed up like a button hole.
Sh!

OLD MAN PECK (*singing in a high, thin voice*)
'Twas just before brave Custer's charge,
Two soldiers drew the rein,
In parting words and clasping hands,
They may never meet again.

One had blue eyes and curly hair,
Just nineteen years ago,
With rosy cheeks and down on his chin,
He was only a boy, you know.

The other was a tall and a dark slim form
With eyes that glittered like gold,
With coal-black hair and brown moustache,
Just twenty-five years old.

The tall dark form was the first to speak,
Saying, "Charley, our hour has come,
We will ride together up on yonder's hill,
But you must ride back alone.

"We have rode together on many a raid,
We have marched for many a mile,
But, comrade dear, I fear the last
Has come with a hopeless smile.

"I have a face, it's all this world to me,
And it shines like a morning's light,
Like a morning's light it has been to me
To cheer my lonesome life.

"Like a morning's light it has been to me
To cheer my lonesome life,
And little did I care for the flow of fate
When she promised to be my wife.

"Write to her, Charley, when I am gone,
Send back this fair-formed face,
And gently tell her how I died
And where is my resting place.

"And tell her I'll meet her on the other shore,
In the bordering land between
Yes, heaven and earth, I'll meet her there,
And it won't be long, I mean."

Then tears filled the eyes of the blue-eyed boy
And his kind heart filled with pain—
"I'll do your bidding, my comrade dear,
Though we never meet again.

"If I get killed and you ride back,
You must do as much for me,

For I have a praying mother at home,
She is all the world to me.

"She has prayed at home like a waiting saint,
She has prayed both night and morn,
For I was the last the country called,
She kissed and sent me on."

Just then, the orders came to charge,
An instant with clasped hands,
Then on they went, then on they rode,
This brave and devoted band.

They rode till they come to the crest of the hill
Where the Indians shot like hail,
They poured death's volley on Custer's men,
And scalped them as they fell.

They turned from the crest of the bloody hills
With an awful gathering gloom,
And those that were left of the faithful band
Rode slowly to their doom.

There was no one left to tell the blue-eyed girl
The words that her lover said,
And the praying mother will never know
That her blue-eyed boy is dead.

[*The crowd applauds and exclaims.*

CROWD
    Shore a good un!

Sings plumb like a church choir, don't he?
Whur's Curly McClain?
Git him to sing.
Here you, Curly, you c'n sing—one of them cow-
puncher ones.

CURLY (*appearing from the crowd*)

Well. Hand me down that guitar, will you?
[*Someone gets the guitar off the cabinet, and hands
it to him. He drags forward a stool and sits down.*

CROWD

"Railroad Man."
"Levee Dan."
"Whistlin' Rufus."
"The Girl I Left Behind Me."
"The Pore Lost Dogie."
"Shoot the Buffalo."
Sump'n lively!
"The Mohawk Trail."

CURLY (*he strums a few notes, and begins to sing, very
simply*)

There is a lady, sweet and kind,
Was never face so pleased my mind,
I did but see her passing by,
And yet I love her till I die.

Her gestures, motion, and her smiles,
Her wit, her voice, my heart beguiles,
Beguiles my heart I know not why,
And yet I love her till I die.

Cupid is wingèd and doth range
Her country so my love doth change,
But change she earth or change she sky,
Yet will I love her till I die.

CROWD (*applauding*)

Sing another'n, Curly.
You shore fooled us. Funny song fer *you* to be a-
singin'!
Now, Aunt Eller—
Aunt Eller, come on, you, it's yore time.

AUNT ELLER

Ketch me a-singin'! Got a frog in my throat—I'm
t'ard, too. Got a ketch in my leg and cain't sing.
Land's alive! Whyn't you git Ado Annie—? Here,
Ado Annie, sing one of them songs of your'n.
[*They drag* ADO ANNIE *forward, squirming.*

CROWD

Here, quit it a-pullin' back, you don't git out of it—

ADO ANNIE (*awkwardly, standing first on one foot, then
on the other*)

Done forgot! Done forgot!

CROWD

Well, hurry up and remember—

ADO ANNIE

Don't know none, nary a one. Done forgot ever one,
I tell you!

CROWD

Well, whistle then, you got to do sump'n.

AUNT ELLER

Forgot yer foot! Sing that un about when you was young and single—

ADO ANNIE

Shoot! My th'oat's plumb sore—

AUNT ELLER

Sump'n else 'll be sore you don't start. Hurry up, now—

ADO ANNIE (*singing in a flat mournful voice*)

When I was young and single,
At home by my own f'ar side,
With my loving brother and sister,
My mother she never would chide.

Then there came a young man
His smiles enticèd me.
—And I was young and foolish
And easy led astray.

I don't see why I love him,
He does not keer for me,
But my thoughts are alwys of him
Wherever he may be.

They tell me not to believe him,
Say "He don't keer fer you."
How little I think that ever
Them words would ever come true!

Some say that love is pleasure.
What pleasure do I see?
For the one I love so dearly
Has now gone back on me!

The night is dark and dreary,
A little incline to rain—
O God, my heart is weary
For my lover's gone off on a train!

OLD MAN PECK

All out fer the smoke-house now! Git some ice cream
in you, you feel better! Got vanilla and strawberry
both, so don't be bashful!
[*The crowd begins to stream noisily out, disappear-
ing past the corner of the house.*

LAUREY (*catching* CURLY *away from his partner, and
dragging him back till the others are all gone*)
Curly!

CURLY (*astonished*)
Now what on earth is ailin' the belle of Claremore?
By gum, if you ain't a-cryin'!
[LAUREY *runs over to him, leans against him.*

LAUREY
Curly—I'm 'fraid, 'fraid of my life—!

CURLY (*in a flurry of surprise and delight*)
Jumpin' toadstools! (*He waves his hat, then throws
it away wildly, and puts his arms around* LAUREY,
muttering under his breath.) Great Lord—!

LAUREY

Don't you leave me—

CURLY

Great Godamighty—!

LAUREY

Don't mind me a-cryin', I cain't he'p it—

CURLY

Jesus! Cry yer eyes out—!

LAUREY

Oh, I don't know whut to do!

CURLY

Here. I'll show you. (*He lifts her face and kisses her. She puts her arms about his neck. He exclaims softly.*) Laurey, Laurey—!
[*He kisses her again and again, then takes a step away from her, disengaging her arms gently.*

LAUREY (*in alarm*)

Curly—

CURLY

My goodness! (*He shakes his head as if coming out of a daze, gives a low whistle, and backs away.*) Whew! 'Bout all a man c'n stand in public—! Go 'way from me, *you!*

LAUREY

Oh, you don't like me, Curly—

CURLY

Like you? My God! Git away from me, I tell you, plumb away from me!
[*He strides across the room and sits down on the stove.*

LAUREY (*crying out*)

Curly! You're settin' on the stove!

CURLY (*leaping up*)

Godamighty! (*He turns round, puts his hand down gingerly on the lids.*) Aw! 'S cold 's a hunk of ice!
[*He sits down again.*

LAUREY (*pouting*)

Wish 't ud burnt a hole in yer pants—

CURLY (*grinning at her, understandingly*)

You do, do you?

LAUREY (*turning away, to hide her smile*)

You heared me.

CURLY

Laurey, now looky here, you stand over there right whur you air, and I'll set over here—and you tell me whut you wanted with me.

LAUREY (*grave again*)

Well— Jeeter was here. (*She shudders.*) He skeered me—he's crazy. I never saw nobody like him—

CURLY (*harshly*)

Whut'd he do? Aunt Eller told me all about the way

you felt—whyn't you tell *me*—why didn't you? Whut'd he do?

LAUREY

Tried to kiss me— Wouldn't let me out of here. Said he'd tried to see me all by myself fer months. He talked wild—and he threatened me.

CURLY

The bastard!

LAUREY

I f'ard him! Told him not to come on the place again. I got mad to see him standin' there like a black cloud, and I told him what! I wish 't I hadn't-a! They ain't no tellin' whut he'll do now! 'F I'd jist a-kep' my head! Now whut am I gonna do!

CURLY

You f'ard him?

LAUREY

Yes, but—

CURLY

Well, then! That's all they is to it! He won't do nuthin'! Tomorrow, I'll git you a new h'ard hand. I'll stay on the place myself tonight, 'f you're nervous about that hound-dog. (*Putting an end to it.*) That's the end of Jeeter, and about time. Now quit yer worryin' about it, er I'll spank you. Hey, while I I think of it—how—how 'bout marryin' me?

LAUREY (*flustered*)

Gracious, whut'd I wanta marry *you* fer?

CURLY (*getting down off the stove and going to her, gravely, like a child*)

Laurey, please, ma'am—marry me. I—I don't know whut I'm gonna do if you—if you don't.

LAUREY (*touched*)

Curly—why, you—why, I'll marry you—'f you want me to—

CURLY (*he takes her in his arms, kisses her gently*)

I didn't think you would, I didn't dream you'd ever—!

LAUREY

Sh!

[*He leads her over, and lifts her up on the stove. Then he lets down the oven door and sits on it, at her feet.*

CURLY (*humbly*)

I ain't got no right to ast you—a good-fer-nuthin' cowpuncher like me—

LAUREY

Don't say things like that.

CURLY

If I'd ever a-thought—! Oh, I'd orta been a farmer, and worked hard at it, and saved, and kep' buyin' more land, and plowed and planted, like somebody— 'stid of doin' the way I've done! Now the cattle busi-ness'll soon be over with. The ranches are breakin' up fast. They're puttin' in barbed w'ar, and plowin' up the sod fer wheat and corn. Purty soon they won't

be no more grazin'—thousands of acres—no place
fer the cowboy to lay his head.

LAUREY

Don't you worry none, Curly—

CURLY

Yer paw done the right way. He knowed. He could
see ahead.

LAUREY

But Pap ain't alive now to enjoy it. But we're alive,
Curly. Alive! Enjoy all we can! Case things happen.

CURLY

Nuthin' cain't happen now—nuthin' bad—if you—if
you love me—and don't mind a-marryin' me.

LAUREY

Sh! I'll marry you. Somebody's comin', don't you
reckon?

CURLY

I don't keer. When *will* you marry me?

LAUREY

Oh, purty soon. I'll have to ast Aunt Eller, first.

CURLY

I'll ast her myself! (*Gaily.*) Oh, I 'member the first
time I ever seen you! You was pickin' blackberries
long side the road here years and years ago—you
was a little tyke. (*He laughs.*) You'd been a-eatin'
berries as fast as you could pick 'em, and yer mouth
was black as a coal shovel!— 'F you wasn't a sight!

LAUREY (*embarrassed*)

Curly!

CURLY

Nen I seen you onct at the Fair—a-ridin' that little gray filly of Blue Starr's, and I says to someone— "Who's that little thing with a bang down on her forehead?"

LAUREY

Yeow, I 'member. You was ridin' broncs that day, and one th'owed you.

CURLY

Did *not* th'ow me!

LAUREY

Guess you jumped off, then.

CURLY

Shore I jumped off.

LAUREY

Yeow, you shore did!

CURLY (*lyrically, rapturously*)

Anh, and I seen you once—the Sunday a year ago, I'll never forget. I come over to break them broncs. You'd been out a-pickin' flowers next to that sorghum mill standin' in the cane patch. And you had a whole armful of Sweet Williams and wild roses and mornin' glories, and I don't know what all. My, I nearly fell off my horse a-lookin' at you! And I thought to my- self—"if this yere bronc th'ows me, I won't land

anywhurs near no Sweet Williams and wild roses.
No sir! No sich luck! I'll find myself 'th my face
plowin' up a patch of cuckle burrs and jimson weeds
—er most likely a ole cow pile!"—

LAUREY

Curly! The way you talk!

CURLY (*as before*)

Be the happiest man a-livin', soon 's we're married!
(*Frowning.*) Oh, but I'll shore be a unsettled man,
though, you're so blame purty, worried somebody'll
run off with you! 'F I ever have to leave home to be
gone all day, gonna shore tie you up to the hitchin'
post, so you'll be there 'gin I git back, you hear?
(*He shakes her playfully.*) Ain't gonna take no
chances! (*Mischievously.*) And looky here, whut're
you gonna give me fer a weddin' present? Well, you
gonna marry a good-fer-nothin' cow hand, 'thout a
red cent in his breeches, 's yer own fault, they come
high! How 'bout a pair of spurs? Er a nice new
saddle blanket, eh, 'th red stripes onto it, and 'nitials
stitched inside of a bleedin' heart on the corner?
Whut's the use of gettin' married, don't git a saddle
blanket er sump'n purty out of it!—

LAUREY

Curly! Now I'll know why you married me—to git a
saddle blanket!

CURLY

Yeow, out in the open, that's me! A man's got to
watch out fer hisself even 'f he has to marry him a

homely critter like you—'th a face like a windmill, make you dizzy to look at it! Come 'ere and kiss me, why don't you?

LAUREY (*gravely, touching his hair shyly*)

I jist set here and listen at you, and don't keer whut you say about me. Say I'm homely 's a mud fence, you want to—why then, I *am* homely 's a mud fence. 'F you say I'm purty, why I'm purty as anything, and got a voice like Jenny Lind. I never thought of anything like this! But I always wondered and wondered, after the first time I ever seen you— (*Her eyes fill with tears, absurdly.*) And here we set, you and me, on the kitchen stove like a pair of skillets, and I don't know whut's come over us to act so silly —and I'm gonna cry in a minute—and it's all yore fault, you orten't to a-made love to me this-a-way—
[CURLY *jumps up, puts his arms around her.*

CURLY

Laurey— Cry 'f you want to, then. (*He kisses her tenderly.*) Laurey, sweet— (*After a moment.*) Now, then. (*Crying out, suddenly.*) Why, my lands of goodness! I plumb forgot! You ain't had nothin' to eat! No pop-corn er ice cream er nuthin'! You pore thing! Wait a minute. I'll git you sump'n 'fore it's all gone! (*He runs and looks down the well, and comes back quickly very much amused.*) Hey! Look in the cupboard there and see 'f you cain't find two glasses. [*He goes back to the well and can be seen hauling up a rope.*

LAUREY

Whut're you up to, Curly?

[*She flies to the cupboard, finds some glasses.* CURLY *has drawn up a small tin bucket, detached it from the rope, and come back, the bucket dripping. He sets it down on the stool, takes off the cover.*

CURLY

Cream! Good ole rich cream, right outa the well! Cold as ice! Freeze yer wish-bone, might' nigh, a-slidin' down yer throat!

[LAUREY *brings the glasses. He pours them full. They are drinking when the* CROWD, *already paired off, sweeps down into the yard hilariously.*

CROWD (*calling out in excitement*)

Hey! Whut's this!

Two little love birds!

Jist a-dyin' to git on the nest, too, from the look of 'em!

Gonna be a weddin'—

Gonna be a shivoree—

How'd a girl ever take to a feller like you, Curly?

AUNT ELLER (*appearing*)

Land sakes, I feel turrible! I went and ketched me a feller and here he is makin' up to another girl!

A MAN

Let's start the lovin' couple off right!

[JEETER *has leaned against a post and stands brood-
ing. He has been drinking and has a bottle in his hand.*

JEETER (*with dark scorn*)

Yay, start 'em off right! To the bride and groom—
[*He lifts the bottle, darkly, insultingly, and hurls
it across the yard, where it breaks with a loud crash.*
CURLY *starts toward him angrily,* LAUREY *clinging to
him.* OLD MAN PECK, *seeing the situation, grabs the
hands of the people nearest him, and they form a
circle which quickly grows, shunting* CURLY *and*
LAUREY *off from* JEETER *on one side of the yard.
Someone begins to sing; the crowd joins in.* LAUREY
and CURLY *are hoisted up on chairs, the circle around
them.*

CROWD (*singing*)

Gone again, skip to my Lou,
Gone again, skip to my Lou,
Gone again, skip to my Lou,
Skip to my Lou, my darling!

Cain't git a redbird, bluebird'll do,
Cain't git a redbird, bluebird'll do,
Cain't git a redbird, bluebird'll do,
Skip to my Lou, my darling!

My girl wears a number ten shoe,
My girl wears a number ten shoe,
My girl wears a number ten shoe,
Skip to my Lou, my darling!

Flies in the buttermilk, two by two,
Flies in the buttermilk, two by two,
Flies in the buttermilk, two by two,
Skip to my Lou, my darling!

CURTAIN

SCENE FIVE

A July moon is over the hayfield, making silver tents of the mounds of unbaled hay which recede in irregular formation far into the distance, crossing a low hill. A gaunt wire rake with enormous wheels stands at one side. The sky is powdered with stars, but low clouds drift often in front of them and the moon, blotting out the stubble. A soft summer wind, creeping about the meadow, lifts the spears of grass that have escaped the sickle. A low hay stack, very near, has a ladder leaning against it.

After a moment, CURLY *and* LAUREY *steal into sight, looking around cautiously. They stop, move forward a little, breathless, begin to speak in hushed voices.*

CURLY (*softly*)
D'you hear anything?

LAUREY (*softly*)
No.

CURLY
Listen. (*They listen. Then he turns to her with relief.*) Not a sound. We've give 'em the slip.

LAUREY
Sh! Whut was that?
[*There is not a sound.*

117

CURLY

Don't hear nuthin'.

LAUREY (*relieved*)

Jist the wind, I guess.

CURLY

Listen. We'll leave Old Eighty standin' whur we tied her. We cain't drive up to the house, 'cause 'f anybody's watchin' out fer us, they'd see us. We'll sneak acrost the hayfield and th'ough the plum thicket— and go in the back door. Come on now. Watch whur you step.

LAUREY (*taking his hand, stopping him, hesitantly*)

Curly,—if they ketch us, whut'll happen? Will it be bad?

CURLY (*soberly*)

You know about shivorees, honey. They git purty rough.

LAUREY

I'm afeard.

CURLY

Don't be afeard, honey. Aunt Eller says fer shore nobody seen us gittin' hitched.

LAUREY

They mighta s'pected sump'n, though. (*Her voice low.*) That's the ketch about gittin' married—

CURLY (*reassuringly*)

But here we air, honey. Married—and purt' nigh home. And not a soul in sight.

LAUREY (*after a moment of registering this, relievedly*)

Yeah. We fooled 'em, didn't we?

CURLY

Shore we did.

LAUREY

Course. (*Her voice full of wonder.*) Curly—we're—we're married now.

CURLY (*softly*)

Yeah. Plumb hitched.

LAUREY

Was you skeered when the preacher said that about "Will you take this here womern—"?

CURLY

Skeered he wouldn't *say* it.

LAUREY

I was skeered you'd back out on me.

CURLY

I *couldn't* back out on you—'f I *wanted* to. Could you *me?*

LAUREY (*smiling tenderly*)

Not if I tried and tried.

[*They kiss, and embrace for a moment. Then still holding her hand,* CURLY *turns, looking out over the moonlit field.*

CURLY (*lyrically, feeling the moment*)

Look at the way the hayfield lays out purty in the moonlight. Next it's the pasture, and over yander's the wheat and the corn, and the cane patch next, nen the truck garden and the timber. Ever'thing laid out fine and jim dandy! The country all around it —all Indian Territory—plumb to the Rio Grande, and north to Kansas, and 'way over east to Arkansaw, the same way, with the moon onto it. Trees ain't hardly a-movin'. Branch bubbles over them limestone rocks, you c'n hear it. Wild flower pe'fume smellin' up the air, sweet as anything! A fine night fer anyone to remember fer a weddin' night! A fine night—fer anyone.

[*Caught up in the spell of the night and their feelings, they move softly away across the stubble, and disappear. There is a moment of silence.*

[*Then there is a subdued titter, followed by shishing sounds, then more titters and smothered laughter. There pop into sight on top of, and from behind the stacks, dozens of men carrying noise-making instruments—tin lids, pots, washboilers, cow bells, gourd rattles, tambourines, pans, iron triangles, whistles, drums. They are an excited, huddled, whispering group, nervous at their long wait for the return of the bride and groom from town, disturbed and hysterical with conjecture on the marital scene they have come to despoil. Veterans of the "shivoree," hardly a bridal couple within twenty miles around, for years and years, has escaped their bawdy ministrations. They look off toward the retreating and oblivious couple, holding their voices down.*

1ST MAN

Sh! They'll hear you!

3RD MAN (*satirically, mockingly*)

"Fine night to remember fer a weddin' night!"
[*Laughter.*

5TH MAN

Fine night fer anyone! Whee! (*Hushing them.*)
Quiet down now! They'll hear you 'fore they git to
the house!

9TH MAN

Tee hee! Bet they'll go to bed in the dark!
[*Laughter.*

10TH MAN (*severely*)

Be keerful! They'll hear us, you hoodlums!

1ST MAN

Sh!

7TH MAN

Cain't you keep yer mouth still a minute!

3RD MAN

Whee! High ole doin's!

5TH MAN

Ketch 'em in the act!

YOUNG FARMER

Whut're we waitin' fer?

OLD FARMER

Give 'em time to git to the house, cain't you?

CORD ELAM

Don't want to give 'em too much time!

10TH MAN

Wish't I uz in his shoes. Godamighty!

3RD MAN

He shore got him sump'n there!

1ST MAN

Couple of sections!

2ND MAN

Grazin' and timber and plowed land!

4TH MAN

Money!

6TH MAN

Scads of it in the bank, and more comin'!

5TH MAN

And God! She's a purty un, too!

3RD MAN

Got a face fer kissin'!

7TH MAN

Hands white as snow!

5TH MAN

And that ain't all, brother!

YOUNG FARMER

No, and that ain't all! Jesus! Wish't I uz in Curly's shoes! 'F I uz Curly, ud be in my bare feet by this time!

1ST MAN (*in great excitement*)

Look! They's a light!

[*The crowd in an excited frenzy begins jumping off the stacks.*

3RD MAN

In the bedroom!

4TH MAN

Look at the way them curtains blow!

2ND MAN

Lace curtains!

3RD MAN

Blowin' out like a shirt-tail a-poppin' in the breeze!

CORD ELAM

Wonder whut they're a-seein', them curtains?

1ST MAN

Bridal couple! Onct in a life-time—

3RD MAN

By theirselves!

4TH MAN

Night come on!

YOUNG FARMER

Ay, the good ole black night—'th nobody to spy on you, nobody to see whut you're up to!

8TH MAN

Look at them shadders a-movin'!

1ST MAN

It's them, they're there! See that *there* un!

2ND MAN

Gittin' ready!

3RD MAN

Got to hurry now, 'come on! Give 'em a s'prise!

CORD ELAM

Don't fergit now, right by this here stack whur the ladder is, like we said!

3RD MAN

Don't make so goddamned much noise!
[*They go out. An* OLD MAN *stumbles into the moonlight, shaking his head, dismally.*

OLD MAN

Listen at that ole owl a-hootin' in the timber, and that there coyote away off yander towards the Verdigree River!
[*He goes out.*
[*A* YOUNG FARMER, *flushed and drinking, staggers darkly out of the gloom.*

YOUNG FARMER

Bridegroom a-waitin' and a-waitin'! Don't you wait now, Mr. Bridegroom! The moon's a-shinin'! Yer time has came! Yes, sirree, bob! No time to wait now. Time to git goin'. See that there bride a-glimmerin' there in her white! Waitin' fer you. Been a-standin' there with her hair down her back and her lips a-movin'! Git next to her, brother! Gonna be high ole times, gonna be Jesus into yer heart!
[*The sound of raucous noise and excitement begins.*

CORD ELAM *runs from around a stack shoving the*
YOUNG FARMER *out of the way.*

CORD ELAM

Git outa the way now, Homer! (*To the approaching
noisy party.*) Hey! Over this-a-way. Yere's the place!
[*The noise of the shivoree grows louder and louder.
Voices rise out of the bedlam, in sharp exclamations
and cries.*
[*A few men drag* CURLY *in, struggling and angry,
his hair in his eyes. His shirt has been ripped off in
the struggle.*

CURLY

God damn you, leave her alone! Don't ary son of a
bitch put his hands onto her, I'll kill him—!

A MAN

Aw, nobody's a-hurtin' her, Curly—

CURLY

Better hadn't. I tell you. Make 'em git away from her,
plumb away from her!

A MAN (*shouting off*)

Git away from her, you all! Bring her on in!
[CURLY *relaxes, but his captors still hold him tightly.*
[*A wide circle of men, shouting, whistling, beating
their various noise implements, advances across the
stubble. In the middle of the group, walking alone,
pale and shaken is* LAUREY, *in a nightgown, her hair
down about her shoulders. The crowd goes over to
the foot of the ladder and stops.*

5TH MAN

Quiet down now, a minute! (*To* LAUREY.) Right up
the ladder with you, you purty thing!
[*The noise stops.*

6TH MAN

Go on, boost her up!

7TH MAN

Right up on the stack—!

8TH MAN

Make out it's a bed, why don't you!
[LAUREY *looks around at* CURLY, *then climbs up the
short ladder, the crowd shouting at her.*

9TH MAN

Watch it!

10TH MAN

Put yer foot in the right place.

CORD ELAM

Don't wanta fall and break yer neck—cheat pore
Curly outa his rights!

10TH MAN

All right, Curly—

6TH MAN

You're next.

10TH MAN

Bring him on over here.
[THE MEN *holding* CURLY *lead him over to the foot*

of the ladder, and let go of him. THE CROWD *begins to call out in more jubilant, crazier derision.*

1ST MAN

Go, on, Mr. Bridegroom, there's yer bride!—

3RD MAN

Purty's a new bronc a-standin' and a-lookin', cain't hardly keep off her!

7TH MAN

Mane like silk and eyes a-shinin'!

CORD ELAM

Git on, there, cowpuncher—! (*After a moment,* CURLY *starts up the ladder, the crowd continuing to shout.*) 'F you ain't a world-beater fer bashful!

3RD MAN

Better be glad we didn't ride you on no fence rail!

1ST MAN

Th'ow the ladder down when he gits up.

10TH MAN

Try to git off, you'll break yer neck, so watch out! [CURLY *reaches the top. Someone throws the ladder down.*

CURLY (*deeply troubled*)

Laurey, honey— (*She looks at him, in dumb misery.*) I'd give my eye-sight, honey—! Try to stand it—I done all I could. I cain't he'p it—
[*He takes her in his arms. The men break out into derisive and lascivious guffaws, and begin the deafen-*

ing noises again, circling the hay stack, kicking up
their heels, in an orgy of delight.

3RD MAN

Give us a little kiss, honey lamb, do a man good, taint
a-askin' much!

CORD ELAM

Give us a lick and a promise!—Quick's these bad ole
mens goes away,—they ain't no a-tellin', no, siree!

5TH MAN

'Taint right to stand there like that— Blush to look
at you!

7TH MAN

Ain't no right to be in no nightgown!

10TH MAN

Go on, Mr. Moon Man, hide yer face fer shame!

YOUNG FARMER

How's it feel to be married, Laurey, sugar, all safe
and proper, to sich a fine purty man with curly hair
and a dimple on his chin! Whee! Got you whur I
want you—!

1ST MAN

Scrunch you to death, purt' near!

CORD ELAM

Bite them shoulders—

3RD MAN

Eat 'er alive!

5TH MAN

Yay, Curly, and it's one more river to cross!
[*One of the men cries out, excitedly, snickering.*

A MAN

Hey, Curly! Hey, Laurey! One baby! (*He tosses a grotesque straw baby high in the air and onto the stack.*) *Two!* (*He tosses another quickly.*) *Three!*
[*He tosses another.*

ANOTHER MAN (*holding up admonishing hands, grinning delightedly*)

Hold it! Not so many! That'll give Curly *idys, that will*!
[*There is raucous laughter, and beating of instruments.*
[*The glow and smoke of something burning which has already crept quietly over the hayfield, now leaps up. A hay stack is burning.*

CURLY (*startled, pointing*)

Look! Fer God's sake, that hay stack's on fire! (THE MEN *rush toward it.*) Get us a ladder someone, quick! The whole hayfield 'll be on fire!
[*Suddenly a dark figure comes into sight, carrying a flaming torch. It is* JEETER.

JEETER (*crying out*)

Yanh, you thought you had it over me so big, didn't you? And you, too, Missy! Wanted sump'n purtier to sleep with. Yanh, you won't be a-havin' it long. Burn you to cracklin's!

[*He springs forward like a maddened animal to apply the torch to the stack.* LAUREY *screams.* THE MEN *start rushing back, as* CURLY *leaps down, knocking the torch out of* JEETER'S *hand.*

CURLY

Godamighty!
[*They struggle.*
[*The crowd exclaims.*

1ST MAN

It's Jeeter Fry! Thought he'd flew the country!

3RD MAN

Drunk as a lord—

3RD MAN

Godamighty, he's crazy drunk!

5TH MAN

He was sweet on her too, they tell me. Stop him, somebody!

7TH MAN

Man seen him last week 'way off in Joplin.

8TH MAN

Jeeter, you goddamned—
[A MAN *beats at the torch with his bare hands, till* ANOTHER MAN *runs up and smothers it quickly with his coat. Someone picks up the torch, stamping out the flames, and runs out to the branch with it.*
[JEETER *has backed away in the struggle, and drawn out a knife. He throws himself upon* CURLY. *The crowd mutters in excitement and fear. The men*

*struggle over the knife, their arms gripping each
other desperately. Suddenly,* JEETER *trips and they
go down on the stubble.* JEETER *groans and whimpers
and lies very still.*

CURLY

Now, now—Christ— (*He shakes his hand, crazily,
helplessly, in horror.*) Look at—look at him! Fell on
it— Stuck it th'ough his ribs!
[*He backs away, shaken, horrified. Some of* THE MEN
bend over the prostrate man.

YOUNG FARMER

Pull that knife out!

MEN

What's the matter?
Don't you tech it!
Turn him over—
He's breathin', ain't he?
Feel his heart.
How'd it happen?

9TH MAN (*wildly*)

Anh, it's went right th'ough his heart—

4TH MAN

Whut'll we do? Ain't he all right?

10TH MAN

'S he jist stunned?

CORD ELAM (*pushing into the crowd*)

Git away, some of you! Lemme look at him. (*He
bends down, the men crowding around.* CURLY *has*

slumped back against the stack, like a sick man.
LAUREY *stands dazed, watching. After a moment,*
standing upright.) Cain't do a thing now. Try to
git him to a doctor, but I don't know—

9TH MAN (*hysterically*)

Pull the knife out, cain't you? Leave a knife stuck
in a—!
[*He springs forward.*

CORD ELAM (*grabbing him*)

You can't pull it out, you fool! Git away from there!
(*The man staggers away, weakly.*) Here, you, some
of you! Carry him down to the branch. Quick! I'm
'fraid it's too late!
[*The men lift* JEETER *up.*

10TH MAN

Handle him easy!

6TH MAN

Don't shake him!

3RD MAN

Hold on to him careful, there!

5TH MAN

Godamighty! Whut a thing to happen!
[*They carry him out.*

CORD ELAM (*to* CURLY)

I don't know, Curly. You better give yerself up, I
'spect. They ain't no a-tellin'. You better go in with
me, as I go, and tell 'em how it was. Tonight. It might

go hard with you, you don't. (CURLY *stands dazed, as if unhearing.*) 'D you hear me, Curly? You know the way ever'body feels about shivoreein'. You got to take it right.

CURLY (*in desperation*)

But f'ar—*f'ar!* He was tryin' to burn us up!

CORD ELAM

I know. But you got to tell the *law*. It'll be easier that way. I'll come back fer you.
[*He goes out toward the branch.*

LAUREY (*in a fever of horror*)

Curly, Curly—

CURLY (*hardly able to speak*)

Laurey—

LAUREY

Is he—is he—?

CURLY

Don't say anything—

LAUREY

It cain't be that-a-way!

CURLY

I didn't *go* to.

LAUREY

Cain't be! Like that—to happen to us!

CURLY

Sh! Be quiet!

LAUREY

Whyn't they do sump'n? Why'd they let him—lay there—? Cain't git over the way he—

CURLY

Laurey, Laurey!

LAUREY (*in mounting hysterical feeling*)

He laid there in the stubble, so quiet, 'th his eyes open, and his eyeballs white and starin'! He laid there in the stubble—'th his eyes open—!

[*She buries her face in her hands, shuddering.*

[CURLY *turns away, numb, speechless, his shoulders hunched up, like one shielding himself from the wind. The howl of a coyote drifts in on the summer air—near and desperate and forlorn.*

CURTAIN

SCENE SIX

A few nights later ADO ANNIE *and* AUNT ELLER *are sitting in the front room, sewing. An oil lamp makes an amber pool of light about them. The sliding doors are closed, but a thin crack of light comes from underneath.* ADO ANNIE, *with a piece of plaid across her knees, is snipping at it with scissors.* AUNT ELLER *is very busy over a flour sack; she pushes her iron spectacles up off her nose and looks over at* ADO ANNIE.

AUNT ELLER (*in astonishment*)

In the name of Doodlebug—whut *air* you a-doin'?

ADO ANNIE (*looking up from her work*)

Makin' a button-hole, cain't you see?

AUNT ELLER

A *round* button-hole?

ADO ANNIE

Course.

AUNT ELLER (*amused*)

Whyn't you make a square one? Er I tell you—make one looks like a four-leaf clover, why don't you?

ADO ANNIE (*shortly*)

Guess I know how to make button-holes.

AUNT ELLER

Yeah, you shore do. Cuttin' a round hole in that plaid. (*They sew in silence. After a moment* AUNT ELLER *glances up toward the closed door, and says.*) She ain't went to bed yit.

ADO ANNIE

'S nine o'clock about.

AUNT ELLER (*shaking her head*)

Worried about her. She don't eat ner sleep sence Curly was tuck away.

ADO ANNIE

She'll git pore she don't eat.

AUNT ELLER

Well, *course* she'll git pore.

ADO ANNIE

That's whut I said.

AUNT ELLER (*slightly irritated*)

I *heared* you say it.

ADO ANNIE (*blandly*)

Well.

AUNT ELLER

Looky here, Ado Annie Carnes, don't you ever marry.

ADO ANNIE (*self-consciously*)

Gracious, who'd I marry?

AUNT ELLER

Don't you *ever!* I did. And *look* at me. (*Half-seri-ously.*) First yer man—*he'll* die—like mine did. Nen the baby—*she'll* die. The rest of yer younguns'll grow up and marry and leave you, the way mine did. Nen you'll be all by yerself. Time you're old as me, you'll be settin' around, jist the way *I* am, 'th a wooden leg and a bald head, and a-rippin' up old floursacks to make yerself a pair of drawers out of.

[*She holds up her work for* ADO ANNIE *to see.*

ADO ANNIE (*overcome with mirth*)

Hee! Hee!

AUNT ELLER

Trouble shore starts, you git married. Look at Laurey. Better *not* git married, I tell you.

ADO ANNIE

Well, I won't then, if you say so.

AUNT ELLER

Anh, but trouble starts nohow, so you might jist as well *git* married as to *not*.

ADO ANNIE (*bewildered*)

Well, which'll I do, then?

AUNT ELLER

Both! I mean—I don't *keer!* (*Her voice sinking to a grave half-whisper, as she says what is really on her mind.*) They *cain't* stick him—

ADO ANNIE

Stick who?

AUNT ELLER

Curly. They *cain't* stick him. Self-defense. Plain's the
nose on yer face. Wish't they'd git it over with, that's
whut I wish—

ADO ANNIE

Did—did Curly *kill* Jeeter—'th that old knife?

AUNT ELLER

Naw! 'Course not! Jeeter *fell* on his ole knife—and
died. And he *ort* to 'a.

ADO ANNIE

They ain't no fair a-holdin' Curly fer it, then?

AUNT ELLER

'Course it ain't fair! It's jist the law. They got to
have their old hearin' first. Them *town* fools! First
the shivoreein'—that was bad enough. And on top of
it—Jeeter. Now Laurey all broke up, and Curly
settin' in the cooler at Claremore. Shore a happy
weddin', I *must* say. Why, them two ain't *railly married* yit.

ADO ANNIE (*her mouth open*)

Ain't they married, Aunt Eller!

AUNT ELLER

Well, they're married, all right, but they ain't— My,
'f you don't know whut I mean, I shore ain't gonna
tell you! (*She gets up, and goes over to the window.*)
Looks blackened up over yander. "More rain, more
rest, more niggers from the West." Hope it don't come
a rain er a big wind-storm 'th all that forty of wheat

in the shock. Ort to a-stacked it, I reckon. (*She turns back*.) Does yer Maw need you tomorrow, Ado Annie?

ADO ANNIE

Naw, she said I could stay all week, 'f you ud feed me.

AUNT ELLER

I'll feed you, all right. Grease-eye gravy and cracklin' corn-bread! And roas'n'ears. Tomorrow we'll start in to can them peaches—clings and all. 'Spect we better be gittin' to bed. Only, I kinda hate to go to bed 'th Laurey still— (*She taps softly at* LAUREY's *door, and calls gently*.) Laurey—

LAUREY (*after a moment, inside*)

Yes.

AUNT ELLER

Ain't you gone to bed yit, honey?
[*The door slides back and* LAUREY *stands there in the lamplight, looking very pale and changed, years older, a woman now.*

LAUREY

I cain't sleep—so—they ain't no sense in goin' to bed. (*She comes down into the room.*) Whut're you makin', Ado Annie?

ADO ANNIE

Me a dress. Ain't it purty?

LAUREY

Yes. (*Gravely.*) Aunt Eller, did they— Whut *did* they say?

AUNT ELLER

I *told* you, honey. Jist said the hearin' was comin'
up tomorrow. Now, I don't want you to worry about
it no more. They'll let him off, all right, they got to.

LAUREY

Curly ort to a-let me went into Claremore with him
like I wanted to—to testify for him.

AUNT ELLER

Don't you know they wouldn't a-let you say nuthin',
Laurey? You're his wife, ain't you?

LAUREY (*slowly*)

Yes. I'm his wife.

AUNT ELLER

Well.
[LAUREY *sinks back in her chair with a disheartened
little moan.*

LAUREY

Oh, I don't see why—I don't see why—when ever'-
thing was so fine, this had to happen!

AUNT ELLER (*comfortingly*)

Oh, Laurey—now nuthin' ain't happened.

LAUREY (*distressed*)

Ain't no tellin' whut they'll do to him! And he couldn't
he'p it. He *couldn't.* (*Seeing it again.*) It was over in
a minute, and Jeeter lay there—dead. He'd a-killed
Curly. He *tried* to kill him.

AUNT ELLER (*soothingly*)

Now, now—

LAUREY

Why'd they have to th'ow Curly in jail? Anyone could see how it happened—

AUNT ELLER

Shore they could, honey. But you know the way everbody feels about shivoreein'. They got a right to it somehow. And a thing like this a-happenin' in the middle of a shivoree—why, it looks *bad*, that's all. But Curly'll go free. Why, it's only been three days. They jist got to git everthing straight.
[*She gestures to indicate freedom and happiness for them both.*

LAUREY

You shore, Aunt Eller?

AUNT ELLER

Course I am!

LAUREY

I cain't stand to think of Curly bein' in jail!

AUNT ELLER

Why, it won't be no time now, till it's all over with— and forgot.

LAUREY (*strangely, a new element coming into her concern*)

No, *not* over with, *not* forgot. You didn't see. Other things. Things you cain't git outa yer mind.
[*She shudders.*

AUNT ELLER

> What is it, honey?

LAUREY

> Over and over! The way them men done. The things
> they said. Oh—why'd it have to be that-a-way!

AUNT ELLER

> Don't let yer mind run on it. Men is always like that
> at shivorees. Sump'n gits into 'em.

LAUREY

> The one time in a body's life—!

AUNT ELLER

> Sh! I know. It musta been bad.

LAUREY

> Cain't ferget it, I tell you! I've tried and tried!

AUNT ELLER (*gravely, wisely*)

> Don't try, honey. Don't *try*. They's things you cain't
> git rid of—lots of things. Not if you live to be a hun-
> dred. You got to learn. You got to look at all the
> good on one side and all the bad on the other, and
> say: "Well, all right, then!" to both of 'em.

LAUREY (*unheeding*)

> —On top of everthing!—

AUNT ELLER (*with great compassion*)

> Yeah, you've had yer troubles. I know, Laurey. But
> they's been good things, too. Think about that. You
> ain't had to slave away a-workin' fer others, the way

some girls has to do,—things like that. You've had you a good home—

LAUREY (*her mind temporarily diverted to another trouble*)

Paw and maw—

AUNT ELLER

Yeah, right when you needed 'em most, both gone. But you lived on, didn't you? You been happy since, ain't you? Course. You been strong about it. Why, when yer Paw died—and you thought the world of him—you was all by yerself here—and you stood it. When they sent fer me to Pryor, 'fore I could git here, why he was dead, and in his coffin.

LAUREY (*raising her head, and looking back into the room*)

It set right there—on two cheers. The head towards the door.

AUNT ELLER

Yeah. (*Quietly, without self-pity, stating the fact.*) When yore Paw died, and laid there—it was *my brother* in his coffin, too. Oh, and they's lots more, Laurey! I couldn't tell you all. Yer Uncle Jack, the children, both of my sisters, my paw and maw. Troubles thick and fast, you got to put up with. My husband—yer Uncle Jack. When *he* died. 'D you know how? A crazy way to die. No use in it! He'd bought some hogs off Lem Slocum, and they turned out to be full of cholery—and all died. Jack walked over jist acrost the pasture to see Lem about it. Didn't show

up and it got night. I tuck a lantern and went out to
see. When I come to the worm fence, I found him, in
a corner, all huddled down, all bloody from a gun-
shot. Laid there all doubled up—dead—in a patch
of yeller daisies. Lem Slocum musta shot him. I didn't
know *who* done it. All I knowed was—*my husband was
dead.* Oh, lots of things happens to a womern. Sick-
ness, bein' pore and hungry even, bein' left alone in yer
old age, bein' afraid to die—it all adds up. That's the
way life is—cradle to grave. And you c'n stand it.
They's one way. You got to be hearty. You *got* to be.

LAUREY (*moved*)

Oh, Aunt Eller, I'm sich a baby—!

AUNT ELLER

There, there!

LAUREY

Ashamed of myself! I want to be the way you air.

AUNT ELLER (*breaking off*)

Fiddlesticks! *Fat*—and *old?* You couldn't *h'ar* me to
be the way *I* am! Why, in a year's time, you'll git so
t'ard even of lookin' at me, you and Curly'll run me
off the place, 'th a tin can tied onto my tail—
[LAUREY *half-smiles at the spectacle, and leaning
over, gives Aunt Eller an affectionate hug.*

LAUREY (*through tears*)

Oh, whut ud I do 'thout you, you're sich a crazy!—

AUNT ELLER

Shore's you're borned!—

LAUREY

I never could live. I never could. (*Rising, happier.*) I'll go to bed now.

AUNT ELLER

And sleep, huh?

LAUREY (*smiling*)

Tight.

AUNT ELLER

And eat hearty from now on, huh? Fried chicken and everthing?

LAUREY

Tomorrow.

AUNT ELLER

Tomorrow, yer foot! (*She gets an apple out of a basket on the organ.*) Here, eat that.

LAUREY

I don't want it.

AUNT ELLER

Eat it, I said.
[LAUREY *takes it, nibbles at it. A dog begins to bark. They all stop abruptly, listening.*

AUNT ELLER

Now, who could that— (*She stands up, looks at* LAUREY, *questioningly.*) This hour of night—
[LAUREY *stands up, quite still, straight and pale.*

LAUREY

Curly—

AUNT ELLER

Couldn't be Curly, 'th ole Shep a-actin' up like a—
He's stopped barkin'. (*The dog's barks stop suddenly.* AUNT ELLER *goes over to the window.* ADO
ANNIE *has put down her work. All three women are in
a breathless tranced state—suspended, curiously
conjecturing.*) It's pitch black—

LAUREY (*with quiet conviction*)

'S Curly come back.

ADO ANNIE (*with a nervous giggle*)

Ole Shep stopped a-barkin' like he was shot!

AUNT ELLER (*angrily—because of her nervous appre-
hension*)

Sh! Be still, cain't you!

LAUREY

It's Curly!

AUNT ELLER

'Taint *no* one. That dog's jist got the colic, I bet.
(*There is a noise as of someone trying the door.*)
What's that!

ADO ANNIE (*rising*)

I'm goin' home.

AUNT ELLER

Be still. (*She picks up a shovel standing in the fireplace. She calls out sharply.*) Now then. Whoever's
there, answer, and answer quick!
[*The door opens quickly, and* CURLY, *dishevelled and
worn, appears there.*

CURLY

Laurey!

AUNT ELLER (*joyfully*)

Why, it's Curly!

LAUREY

Curly!
[*She runs to meet him half-way across the room as he comes forward. They go into each other's arms, and cling to each other.*

AUNT ELLER (*with extravagant delight*)

My, oh my! Look whut the old cat's drug in! Thought we had him safe in jail and here he turns up like a bad penny! Laws a me! Whutta you mean tryin' to skeer us wall-eyed?

ADO ANNIE (*astonished*)

Why, it's Curly!

AUNT ELLER (*gaily*)

Naw! It's Sandy Claus, cain't you see nuthin'! They've let him off! I knowed they would, I knowed it, I knowed it!
[CURLY *backs out of* LAUREY'S *arms, looks round quickly.*

LAUREY

Curly! Whut is it!

CURLY

Whut was that noise?

LAUREY (*with premonitory alarm*)

Whut's the matter? Everything's all right, ain't it? They've let you off, ain't they? Curly! Tell me and be quick, I—

CURLY

No. They ain't let me off.

LAUREY

Curly! (*Running to him.*) They couldn't a-sent you up! It wasn't yore fault. They couldn't, I won't let 'em—I won't, I—

CURLY

Sh! (*As they become silent.*) They're after me.
[*He goes swiftly across and pulls down the window shade.*

AUNT ELLER

Never heared of sich a— Who's after you, the old Booger Man?

LAUREY

Curly!

CURLY

When I clumb th'ough the fence jist by that little bridge, I seen lights 'way over towards Claremore. I knowed they'd got onto which way I was headin', so I run acrost the back of the—

AUNT ELLER

Whut *air* you jabberin' about? (*Light dawning on her.*) Oh! I mighta knowed a curly-headed cowhand

like him ud come to a bad end! He's went and broke
outa jail.

CURLY (*quickly*)

I *had* to see Laurey. I *had* to! I knowed she'd be
a-worryin' about everthing, and I couldn't stand
it her a-worryin' and nobody to help her none—
[*He takes* LAUREY *in his arms again.*

AUNT ELLER (*severely*)

Worryin'! I ort to take a hick'ry to you and beat you
plumb to a frazzle! Here you'd a-got off tomorrow,
you crazy youngun—everbody *said* so. Now you'll
prob'ly git sent up fer five year fer breakin' loose—
and I hope you do!

LAUREY

Aunt Eller, they cain't send him up, they *cain't!*

AUNT ELLER

Oh, cain't they? You wait and see. (*To* CURLY.) Didn't
you know they'd know whur you was headin' fer, and
find you 'fore a cat could lick his front paw?

CURLY

I didn't think.

AUNT ELLER

I reckon you hain't got nuthin' to think *with*. (*Giving
him a swat.*) I'd like to give you a good beatin'!
(*Smiling at him tolerantly.*) Aw, I reckon you jist
had to see yer girl, didn't you?

CURLY

My wife.

AUNT ELLER

Yeow? Well, *call* her that 'f it does you any good. How fur back was it you seen 'em comin' after you?

CURLY

'Bout half a mile.

AUNT ELLER

You got jist about two minutes to tell Laurey "Good-bye" then.

CURLY

They won't ketch me! Hide me till mornin', Aunt Eller. I cain't let 'em take me now, Aunt Eller!

AUNT ELLER

You'll stay *right* here till they come! You've already caused enough trouble to last us all out to dooms-day. Now then. Ado Annie, come on out in the kitchen, and git yerself sump'n to eat. Bet you're hungry.

ADO ANNIE

I hain't hungry, Aunt Eller. I jist had a piece of—

AUNT ELLER

Not hungry! Why, you're all fallin' to staves. Feel ever' rib you got! (*She shoves* ADO ANNIE *out and follows her. As she goes out.*) They'll come any minute now.

CURLY (*after a moment, not knowing how to begin*)
You all right, honey?

LAUREY

Yes. I guess. (*She puts her hand to her forehead as if brushing away her darkness.*) I git to thinkin'.

CURLY (*gently*)

I know. Me, too. Thinkin' and thinkin' about you—
and be bringin' sich trouble on you. All my fault.

LAUREY

Nobody could he'p it.

CURLY

Listen, Laurey. (*She goes to him, questioningly, disturbed at something in his manner.*) I had to see you
'fore the hearin' tomorrow. That's why I broke out.
Fer whut if they'd send me up, and I not see you fer a
long time?

LAUREY

Curly! It *couldn't* be. Don't you say that.

CURLY

Anything can be. You got to be ready.

LAUREY (*alarmed*)

Have you heared anything, Curly? Tell me, whut'd
you hear?

CURLY

Nuthin', honey. Ain't heared nuthin'—but *good*.

LAUREY (*with glad relief*)

Oh, it's all right, then!

CURLY (*gravely*)

That ain't it. I'm shore myself, honey. Er I *was* shore,
till I broke out. I never thought whut *that* might do.
But sump'n's always happenin' in this here world.
Cain't count on a thing. So you got to promise me

sump'n. Whutever happens—*whutever* it is—you got
to bear up, you hear me? (*Smiling.*) Why, I'm a purty
one to go a-losin' sleep over, ain't I?

LAUREY (*ruefully*)

Oh, a fine start *we* got, ain't it? (*With an effort, pain-
fully working it out in her mind.*) Oh, I've worried
about you, shet up in that filthy jail—

CURLY

Don't mind about that.

LAUREY

—And I've thought about that awful night, too, till
I thought I'd go crazy—

CURLY

Pore Laurey.

LAUREY

Looked at it time and again, *heared* it—ringin' in
my ears! *Cried* about it, cried about everthing! A
plumb baby! And I've tried to figger out how it ud
be if sump'n *did* happen to you. Didn't know how I
could stand it. That was the worst! And nen, I tried
to figger out how I'd go on. Oh, I've went th'ough
it all, Curly, from the start. Now I feel shore of
sump'n, anyway—I'll be growed up—like everbody
else. (*With conviction.*) I'll put up with everthing
now. You don't need to worry about me no more.
Why, I'll stand it—if they send you to the pen fer
life—

CURLY (*with mock alarm*)

Here! Don't know's I like that very well!
[LAUREY *bursts out into a peal of amused, hearty,
infectious laughter.*

LAUREY

The look on yore face! 'S the first time I laughed in
three days!

CURLY (*his old self again*)

I ain't goin' to no pen fer life—a-poundin' up rocks,
and a-wearin' stripes around my legs!

LAUREY

Wouldn't you look purty!

CURLY (*with delight*)

You *air* a devil, ain't you? I don't think you **even**
like me.

LAUREY (*playfully*)

Like you? Oh, I like you a little bit. (*They stand
looking at each other, shyly, happily.*) Whur **on**
earth'd you git them clothes you got on?

CURLY (*gaily*)

Old Man Peck went and got 'em fer me. Shore a good
ole man! Thinks the world of you. Shirt come outa
Rucker's Dry Goods Store. Brand new, too! He
thought I must be a-needin' clean clothes, I reckon,
shet up in that ole jail! My, they's things a-crawlin'
there, got legs on both sides! Cell next to mine's got
a couple of horse thieves into it, the A. H. T. A.

caught up by Sequoyah. They gimme a blanket and one of 'em said, "Tain't so purty-fer-nice but it's hell-fer-warm."

LAUREY (*amused*)

Curly!

CURLY

'Nother cell's got a womern into it that smokes and cusses like a mule driver. Caught her stealin' from the Turf Exchange. Don't know whut's got into Indian Territory nohow! They puttin' everbody in jail—women and all!

LAUREY

I think you like yer ole jail!

CURLY

Jist rairin' to git back. Cain't wait! Lay back on that arn cot and dream about featherbeds!

LAUREY (*softly, happily*)

Ever time I pass by the barn lot, ole Dun lopes acrost and nickers at me, fer all get-out! Shows his teeth. He's astin' about you, I reckon.

CURLY

Oh, he's apt to fall dead of the heaves when he hears about me——settin' in jail 'stid of on the range! Feels like I ain't set in the saddle in a month of Sundays! Listen, Laurey. I been a-thinkin'—— Everthing from now on is gonna be different.

LAUREY

Different?

CURLY

It come to me settin' in that cell of mine. (*Dreamily, out of a visionary absorption—like a song, growing in intensity.*) Oh, I got to learn to be a farmer, I see that! Quit a-thinkin' about dehornin' and brandin' and th'owin' the rope, and start in to git my hands blistered a new way! Oh, things is changin' right and left! Buy up mowin' machines, cut down the prairies! Shoe yer horses, drag them plows under the sod! They gonna make a state outa this, they gonna put it in the Union! Country a-changin', got to change with it! Bring up a pair of boys, new stock, to keep up 'th the way things is goin' in this here crazy country! Life jist startin' in fer me now. Work to do! Now I got you to he'p me— I'll 'mount to sump'n yit! Come here, Laurey. Come here, and tell me "Goodbye" 'fore they come fer me and take me away.

LAUREY (*wryly*)

All we do is say "Howdy" and "So long." (*Gravely.*) Goodbye, Curly. If you come back tomorrow, I'll be here a-waitin'. If you don't come back, I'll be here a-waitin' anyhow.

CURLY

I'll come back, honey. They couldn't hinder me 'th bird-shot!

LAUREY

Promise me.

CURLY

Oh, I hate to go away and leave you! I cain't. (*He*

takes her in his arms, hungrily. After a moment, there are VOICES *and sounds of an approaching party. The couple listen breathlessly.*) They're here. Oh, I cain't go, I cain't leave you!

LAUREY (*anguishedly, clinging to him*)

I cain't let you go.
[AUNT ELLER *comes in.*

AUNT ELLER (*gravely*)

Well, here they air, I guess. They's a whole crowd. I seen the lanterns. You all ready, Curly?

CURLY (*in anguish*)

I guess—I—

AUNT ELLER (*tenderly*)

Goodbye, honey. I'm sorry it has to be like this. (*There is a knock at the door.* AUNT ELLER *goes over and calls, her hand on the latch.*) Who is that a-knockin'?

VOICE (*outside*)

It's me, Ed Peck—and I got to see you about—

AUNT ELLER (*opening the door, in astonishment*)

Why, Mr. Peck! Come on in. Whutta *you* want around here?

OLD MAN PECK (*coming in, his eyes going to* CURLY)

Curly knows whut I want. I've *come* fer him.

AUNT ELLER

You have? You ain't no marshal.

OLD MAN PECK

I know. But Mr. Burnett, the federal marshal, depu-

tized me and some of the boys to come out and find
Curly and bring him back. Come on, Curly.

AUNT ELLER

Well, I *must* say! Sidin' with the federal marshal!

OLD MAN PECK

I ain't sidin' with him, Aunt Eller. Curly's hearin' ain't
come up yit, and he hadn't no right to run off this-
a-way.

AUNT ELLER

No right! Say, looky here, he wanted to see his wife.
That ain't agin the *law* in this country, is it?

OLD MAN PECK

No. But breakin' outa *jail* is agin the law.

AUNT ELLER (*disgusted*)

Well, of all the— When'd you go and git so respectful
of the law? Looky here, if a law's a *good* law—it
can stand a little breakin'. And them out there—
Who's out there? Hey, you all! (*She has gone to the
window and thrown up the shade.*) Go on home. Nobody's wantin' *you* around here!

VOICES (*outside*)

We've come fer Curly, Aunt Eller. We got to take
him back.
(*Snickering.*)
He's a plumb criminal, he is, breakin' outa jail this-a-
way!

AUNT ELLER

Who's that? That you, Zeb? I mighta knowed! Say,

you're a purty nuthin'—a ole pig-stealer like you tryin' to represent the govament!

VOICE (*outside, offended, protesting*)

You're a purty nuthin'—a ole pig-stealer like you tryin' to represent the govament!

VOICE (*outside, offended, protesting*)

Who's a pig-stealer?

AUNT ELLER

You air, Mr. Zeb Walkley.

VOICE

I ain't, either!

AUNT ELLER

You *air!* Why, you gittin' so that—'stid of talkin'— you plumb grunt like a ole sow! And say, Dave Tyler —you'll feel funny when I tell yer wife you're carryin' on 'th another womern, won't you?

VOICE (*outside*)

I ain't carryin' on 'th no one.

AUNT ELLER

Mebbe not. But you'll shore feel funny when I tell yer *wife* you air.

VOICES

Now, Aunt Eller, we've come fer Curly.
We cain't stand here and listen to you—
Send him on out!

AUNT ELLER (*indignantly*)

Oh, you'll listen to me! I'm gittin' mad! You cain't *take* Curly, that's all they is to it!

VOICES

We *got* to, Aunt Eller.

He'll git off tomorrow, won't he?

Make him come on out, and le's git started!

AUNT ELLER (*severely*)

All right, 'f you won't listen to me, I plumb warsh
my hands of all of you. I thought you was a fine bunch
of neighbors. Now I see you're jist a gang of fools.
Tryin' to take a bridegroom away from his bride!
Why, the way you're sidin' with the federal marshal,
you'd think us people out here lived in the United
States! Why, we're territory folks—we ort to hang
together. I don't mean *hang*—I mean *stick*. Whut's
the United States? It's jist a furrin country to me.
And *you* supportin' it! Jist dirty ole furriners, ever
last one of you!

VOICES (*outside, grumbling, protesting*)

Now, Aunt Eller, we hain't furriners.

My pappy and mammy was *both* borned in Indian
Territory! Why, I'm jist plumb full of Indian blood
myself.

Me, too! And I c'n prove it!

AUNT ELLER (*full of guile*)

Well, maybe you *ain't* furriners. I musta made a mis-
take. (*Slyly, smiling.*) Anyway, I ain't astin' you
to let Curly *off*. That's up to them ole United
Statesers at the hearin'. *I* mean—you don't have to
take Curly back *tonight*. Take him in the mornin'
jist as well.

VOICES (*uncertainly*)

Well, I don't know—
I ain't no furriner!
Whut does Mr. Peck say?
He's the boss. Ast *him*.
I wouldn't wanta stand in the way of lettin' Curly—

AUNT ELLER (*triumphantly, to* MR. PECK)

See there! They said it was all right to let him stay
tonight.

OLD MAN PECK

No, they didn't.

AUNT ELLER

Did too! Cain't you hear nuthin'? I'll take a black-
snake whip to you!

OLD MAN PECK (*sheepishly*)

Well, I— If my men is gonna back out on me this-
a-way—I reckon I better let Curly stay.

AUNT ELLER (*overjoyed*)

I knowed you'd see daylight, I knowed it, I knowed it!

OLD MAN PECK (*self-consciously, not looking at* CURLY,
and twirling his hat in his hands, sheepishly)

I was young onct myself.
[*He hugs* AUNT ELLER.

AUNT ELLER

Why, you ole devil! Tell yer wife on you!

CURLY

'D you want me to stay, Laurey?

[*She backs away, flushed and embarrassed and joyous at the same time, flings an arm about his neck and kisses him quickly, whirls over to* OLD MAN PECK, *gives him a quick hug and flies into her room.* CURLY *grins and starts after her.*

OLD MAN PECK (*as* CURLY *reaches the door*)

Curly. I'll be here right after breakfast to fetch you. I'll be here bright and early.

[CURLY *goes in. The door shuts.*

AUNT ELLER (*slyly, owlishly*)

Well, not *too* early. (*Then, gravely.*) Younguns has a turrible time, don't they? (*She throws it off.*) Oh, well—they git to be old timers soon enough. *Too* soon. (*She shows* MR. PECK *out with a lantern. She marches over to the window, calling out.*) Hey, you all! Go on home. They ain't nuthin' *you* c'n do around here. Curly's *stayin'!*

[*She jerks the shade down.*

[*The voices outside exclaim delightedly and move away. From the bedroom has come the sound of* CURLY *beginning to sing softly,* "Green Grow the Lilacs."

AUNT ELLER (*going to the window*)

Mr. Peck! (*With delight.*) Listen to that fool cow-puncher! His weddin' night—and there he is singin'!

CURTAIN

THE END

GLOSSARY

dogies—specifically, an orphaned calf, but used often, affectionately, as a synonym for cattle.

shikepoke—a mythical Middle West bird, whose activities (unprintable) are embarrassing to everyone. A term of opprobrium.

side meat—bacon.

maverick—an unbranded, and hence ownerless, calf or steer.

off-ox—the ox on the off-side (the right side) of the wagon tongue.

bronc buster—a rider of bucking bronchos.

bull-dogger—one who leaps off a running horse, swings on the horns of a bull or steer, and throws and ties him.

stove arn—that is, stove iron, or handle for lifting the lids.

tetchin' leather—to ride a bronc without touching leather is to ride without hanging on to the saddle horn or any other part of the saddle.

yellin' calf-rope—to yell calf-rope signifies defeat.

to change the green lilacs to the red, white and blue—means, "I'm going to join the army."

string-haltered—a corruption of spring-halted, a convulsive movement of the hind legs of a horse.

Dan Patch—a celebrated racing horse, a pacer.

Jick—the joker in a pack of cards.

bottom—that is, river bottom, the low land along a
river.

backwater—the water backed up, from being unable to
empty into a swollen stream now higher than its
tributaries.

shivoree—a corruption of the French *charivari*, a wed-
ding celebration.

the A. H. T. A.—the Anti-Horse Thief Association.

CPSIA information can be obtained at www.ICGtesting.com
Printed in the USA
BVOW02s1028260315

393250BV00012B/160/P

9 780573 609626